THE POLITICAL ANATOMY
OF IRELAND

SIR WILLIAM PETTY

THE POLITICAL ANATOMY OF IRELAND

with the
Establishment for that Kingdom
and Verbum Sapienti

Introduction by
JOHN O'DONOVAN

IRISH UNIVERSITY PRESS
Shannon · Ireland

First edition London 1691

This IUP reprint is a photolithographic facsimile of the first edition and is unabridged even to the extent of retaining the original printer's imprint

SBN 7165 0093 0

Irish University Press Shannon Ireland
DUBLIN CORK BELFAST LONDON NEW YORK

T M MacGlinchey Publisher

PRINTED IN THE REPUBLIC OF IRELAND AT SHANNON
BY ROBERT HOGG PRINTER TO IRISH UNIVERSITY PRESS

INTRODUCTION

During the period of more than 700 years that England was responsible for the government, at first of part and subsequently of the whole of Ireland, the number of outstanding administrators sent to this country could almost be counted on the fingers of one hand. Strangely enough, two of them came in the seventeenth century, Thomas Wentworth, Earl of Strafford and Sir William Petty.

Petty 'sonn of a meane man' according to John Evelyn, the diarist, was born in 1623. At the age of fourteen, while a cabin boy on an English merchant ship, he broke his leg and was put ashore on the French coast near Caen. His account of his misfortunes to the Jesuit fathers of that city was made in such excellent Latin that they not alone took care of him but educated him in their college. He helped towards his maintenance by teaching and by hawking 'pittiful brass things with cool'd glasse in them instead of diamonds and rubies'. He subsequently studied medicine at Amsterdam, Leyden and Utrecht and read with Hobbes in Paris.

On his return to England in 1646, he engaged in many diverse activities without much success until his appointment as deputy to the professor of anatomy at Oxford in 1648. He succeeded the professor in 1650 and about this time became vice-principal of Brasenose College, Oxford, and professor of music at the Gresham College, London.

In 1652, he was appointed physician to the Cromwellian army in Ireland and clerk of the Irish Council. He lived in Ireland nearly seven years, 1652–59, and it was during this period he made the Down Survey of Ireland, which was commissioned in 1654. Its purpose was to facilitate the distribution of the forfeited lands of the rebels of 1641, in equal moieties, among the soldiers of the Cromwellian army and those who had subscribed money for the army's support. Petty himself obtained considerable lands in Kerry. The completion of the survey and work of distribution in a period of four years, despite the deplorable condition of the country, was a remarkable administrative achievement.

On his return to London, Petty was admitted to membership of the Scientific Inquiry Society, which met in Gresham College and from which sprang the Royal Society for Improving of Natural Knowledge, of which he was a founder member.

In 1666, Petty came again to Ireland and during the following years, although kept busy in connection with his lands in Kerry, wrote many works including *The Political Anatomy of Ireland* which is believed to have been written in 1672 but was not published until 1691.

On the accession of James II, whom he knew, he went back to London and tried to obtain the establishment of a Statistical Office for Ireland, under his own supervision, and the reform of the system of farming the collection of taxes. He also wrote a memorandum recommending that the King should treat the Protestants in Ireland carefully. None of these projects came to fruition and Petty died in London in 1687.

Opinions as to Petty's contribution to political economy vary but on the whole the books on the history of economic thought written in recent years give him a good showing. Some great German economists have, however, taken opposite sides. Roscher, the learned leader of the older German Historical School, and Karl Marx both held the view that Petty was the founder of modern economic thought. Schumpeter, the famous German who taught for nearly twenty years at Harvard in the thirties and forties of the present century, maintained that Petty was not an original thinker. Whichever view is taken, there is agreement that he made a substantial contribution to the infant science of statistics. In his own words, he set out to replace 'intellectual argument' by the adoption of 'number, weight and measure' in his approach to the examination of economic phenomena through the collection of social and economic facts and figures.

The Political Anatomy of Ireland contains one of the very first plans set down on paper for the development of an economy and for the provision of employment. Petty can, therefore, be regarded as one of the first econometricians. Some of the suggestions made by him were carried out in the eighteenth century, for example the building of Arus an Uachtaráin in the Pheonix Park and the construction of the Port of Dublin.

John O'Donovan
December 1969 University College, Dublin

THE
Political Anatomy
OF
IRELAND.

WITH
The Eſtabliſhment for that Kingdom when the late Duke of ORMOND was Lord Lieutenant. Taken from the RECORDS.

To which is added
VERBUM SAPIENTI; or an Account of the Wealth and Expences of *England*, and the Method of raiſing Taxes in the moſt Equal manner.
Shewing alſo, That the Nation can bear the Charge of Four Millions *per Annum*, when the occaſions of the Government require it.

By Sir WILLIAM PETTY, late Fellow of the Royal Society, and Surveyor-General of the Kingdom of *Ireland*.

LONDON:
Printed for *D. Brown*, and *W. Rogers*, at the *Bible* without *Temple-Bar*, and at the *Sun* over-againſt St. *Dunſtans* Church, *Fleetſtreet*. 1691.

To His Grace the

Duke of ORMOND.

MY LORD,

THE Celebrated Author of the following Treatise, had not only the Honour to be known to Your Grace's Grand-Father, the late Illustrious Duke of *ORMOND*, but was likewise held by Him in that just Esteem, which he never fail'd of expressing towards Men of Learn-

Learning and Ingenuity. This was a ſufficient Encouragement to me (having the Manuſcript-Copy deliver'd into my Hands by a Worthy and Intimate Friend of the Authors, to diſpoſe of it to the Preſs for the publick Benefit) to Addreſs it to Your Grace's Patronage. You are ſo true a Succeſſor in all the generous Virtues of Your Anceſtry, that I cannot doubt of Your favourable Reception of this Poſthumous Work. Your Generoſity, that takes all occaſions of exerting it ſelf towards the Living, cannot fail in doing

ing Justice to the Memory of the Dead. More especially to such Persons as in their Life took care to oblige Posterity.

The usefulness of the ensuing Discourse at this time, when there is so fair a prospect of a new Settlement in *IRELAND*, were sufficient to recommend it to Your Grace's Protection. Your Grace's Interest in the Re-establishment of that Kingdom (tho it be considerable) yet is much less than your Share in the glorious Enterprize towards its Recovery.

You had the Honour of accompanying His MAJESTY in an Adventure that shall shine in the Annals of *Fame*, as long as the *Boyne* shall maintain its Course. But a single Gallantry appear'd not sufficient for the Heir of ORMOND and OSSERY. You have since accompanied our Royal Master to other Shores, to be partaker with him in new Scenes of Action, Undertakings of no less Consequence and Importance, than the Deliverance of *Europe*. This will afford sufficient matter for Panegyrick, and oblige the Mu-

ses

ses to place you in the same high Rank of Renown with Your Noble and Heroick Predecessors. In the mean time, be pleas'd to permit this useful Treatise to wait on you to the Camp, and bring you the hearty wishes of all good Men here, for Your happy Expedition, and Your safe Return, which is desir'd by none with a more particular Zeal, than by

Your GRACE'S

Most Devoted Servant,

N. TATE.

THE

THE

Author's Preface.

SIR Francis Bacon, *in his* Advancement of Learning, *hath made a judicious* Parallel *in many particulars, between the* Body Natural, *and* Body Politick, *and between the Arts of preserving both in Health and Strength: And it is as reasonable, that as* Anatomy *is the best foundation of one, so also of the other; and that to practice upon the Politick, without knowing the* Symmetry, Fabrick, *and* Proportion *of it, is as* casual *as the practice of Old-women and Empyricks.*

Now, because Anatomy *is not only necessary in Physicians, but laudable in every Philosophical person whatsoever; I therefore, who profess no Politicks, have, for my curiosity, at large attempted* the first Essay of Political Anatomy.

Furthermore, as Students in Medicine, practice their inquiries upon cheap and common Animals, *and such whose actions they are best*

ac-

acquainted with, and where there is the least confusion and perplexure o Parts; I have chosen Ireland *as such a* Political Animal, *who is scarce Twenty years old; where the* Intrigue *of* State *is not very complicate and with which I have been conversant from an* Embrion; *and in which, if I have done amiss, the fault may be easily mended by another.*

'Tis true, that curious Dissections *cannot be made without variety of proper Instruments; whereas I have had only a commin* Knife *and a* Clout, *instead of the many more helps which such a Work requires: However, my rude approaches being enough to find whereabout the Liver and Spleen, and Lungs lye, tho' not to discern the Lymphatick Vessels, the* Plexus, Choroidus, *the* Volvuli *of vessels within the Testicles; yet not knowing, that even what I have here readily done, was much considered, or indeed thought useful by others, I have ventur'd to* begin *a* new *Work, which, when Corrected and Enlarged by better Hands and Helps, I believe will tend to the Peace and Plenty of my Country; besides which, I have no other end.*

A D-

ADVERTISEMENT.

THE *Reader* is desired to take notice; That by *Letterees*, are meant persons restored to Land by virtue of the *Letters* of King *Charles* the Second; and by *Nominees*, such persons are intended, as were restored to their Lands by being *named* in the *Act* of *Settlement*; and Papists *per Proviso*, were such as had *Provisoes* in that *Act* for their Lands: And by *the* 49 *Officers*, are meant such *Commission-Officers* under the King, who served in *Ireland* before the *year* of our *Lord*, 1649.

The following Treatise of Sir *William Petty's Political Anatomy of Ireland*, is Printed after a Copy Transcribed from the *Original*, writ by the *Author*'s own hand; and all the *Blanks*, as here Printed, were in that *Original*: And which, tho' it may be suppos'd he could easily have fill'd up, yet was it not held proper for any other to attempt, or to add to any thing done by so great a *Master*.

This his work of *The Political Anatomy of Ireland* ends in *page* 113.

P. 114.

ADVERTISEMENT.

P. 114. begins the famous *Report* from the *Council* of *Trade* in *Ireland*, which was not only *Drawn*, but wholly *Composed* by Sir *William Petty*; and with which that Council concurred unanimously.

P. 132. followeth the Copy of the *Commission* of the late *Duke of Ormond* to be *Lord Lieutenant*; and an Account of the *Establishment of the Civil and Military List* in his time; faithfully and carefully taken out of Authentick *Records*: And to the Nature of which, the continued *Title* of *The Political Anatomy of* Ireland. on those *Pages*, agrees well enough.

The *Volume* concludes with Sir *William Petty's Verbum Sapienti*, which relates wholly to *England*, and shews how Taxes may be equally laid, and how the Nation may well bear the Tax of Four Millions *per Annum*.

The Reader is now left with his most Critical attentive Judgment, to enjoy the benefit of the great Political knowledg that Sir *William Petty* hath taught the Age; and for which (as one of the greatest Ornaments of it) he deserveth perpetual celebrations. Know *Reader* in a word, That.

Nulla ferent talem sæcla futura virum.

The

The CONTENTS of the Political Anatomy of *IRELAND*.

Of the Lands of Ireland, *with the present distribution and Values of the same.* Page 1
Of the People, Houses and Smokes; their Number, Differences and Values, 7
Of the Church and Benefices. 16
Concerning the late Rebellion and its effects, 17
Of the future Settlement of Ireland, *Prevention of Rebellions, and its Union with* England, 25
Of the Government of Ireland, *Apparent and Internal.* 36
Of the Militia and Defence of Ireland, 42
Of the Cœlum, Solum, & Fruges; *or the Air, Soil and Product of* Ireland, 48
Of the Rate which the Lands in Ireland *do bear to each other, with the History of the several Valuations of the same,* 58
Of the Money of Ireland, *and the Causes of its Decrease, with the Remedy for the same,* 68

Of

The Contents.

Of the Trade of Ireland, *and its Impediments; the Commodities, and aptitude for Traffick, and incidently of the Cloaths and Dyet of the People: Of Sumptuary Laws, Absentees,* &c. 75

Of the Religion, Language, Manners, and Interest of the present Inhabitants of Ireland; *as also of the Present and Ancient Divisions and Names of the Lands,* 93

Some Miscellany Remarques and Intimations concerning Ireland, *and the several matters aforementioned,* 103

A Report from the Council of Trade in Ireland, *to the Lord Lieutenant and Council,* &c. 114

Considerations relating to the Improvement of Ireland, 115

Inferences from the Premises, 120

Propositions to His Majesty concerning the Government of Ireland, 146

The List for Civil Affairs, &c. 157

The Establishment and List, containing all the Payments to be made for Military Affairs, &c. 181.

Officers Provincial, 184

Constables, 186

Sundry Ministers belonging to the Ordnance, viz. *in* Lemster, 188

Con-

Connaught, 189
Munster, 190
Ulster, 191
Temporary Payments, 196
A Catalogue of the Peers, 199
A List of the Arch-Bishopricks and Bishopricks, 200
Barons, 201
A List of those Places that return Parliament-Men, &c. 202

Verbum Sapienti.

Introduction, Page 1
Chap. 1. *Containing several Computations of the Wealth of the Kingdom,* 3
Chap. 2. *Of the Value of the People,* 7
Chap 3. *Of the several Expences of the Kingdom, and its Revenue,* 10
Chap. 4. *Of the Method of apportioning Taxes,* 11
Chap. 5. *Of Money, and how much is necessary to drive the Trade of the Nation,* 13
Chap. 6. *The Causes of Irregular Taxing,* 15
Chap. 7. *The Collateral Advantages of these Taxes,* 16

The Contents.

Chap. 8. *Of the Expence of the Navy, Army, and Garisons*, 18
Chap. 9. *Motives to the quiet bearing of Extraordinary Taxes*, 19
Chap. 10. *How to imploy the People, and the end thereof*, 22

LICENSED, *May* the 11th. 1691.

THE

THE

The Political Anatomy OF IRELAND.

1672.

Of the Lands of Ireland.

THERE are in *Ireland* of Acres of Land, *Irish* Measure (whereof 121 Acres makes 196 *English* Measure) near about	M. Ac. 10,500
Whereof there is of Rivers, Highways, Loughs, unpassable Bogs, Rocks and Shrubs, about	M. 1, 500
Of very course Land, commonly call'd unprofitable	1, 500
Consequently of good Meadow, Arrable and Pasture	7, 500
	10, 500

Of

Of which *Anno* 1641, there did belong to Papists and Sequestred Protestants	5,200
To the Church, *viz.* Bishops, Deans, Chapters and Glebes	300
To the Protestants planted by Queen *Elizabeth* and King *James*	2,000
	7500

Of the 5,200 *belonging to Papists and Sequestred Protestants* Anno 1641.

There was restored to 26 that proved their constant good Affection, *per est.*	40	210
To His Grace the D. of *Ormond.*	130	
To the Lord *Inchiquine*, Lord *Roscommon*, and others	40	
To innocent Papists, near	1,200	
To the Church, near	20	140
To the Duke of *York*, near	120	
To Letterees and Nominees *Irish-men*	60	420
To Papists, *per proviso* with Collonel *Vernon*	360	

Left

Left in the Common-Stock of Courſe-Land	80	470
To Adventurers	390	
To Soldiers ſince 49.	1,440	
To the 49 Officers	280	550
To Proteſtants *per proviſo*	270	
Upon Tranſplantation Decrees	700	
Reſtored to Mortgagees Proteſtants, about	100	
		5,200
So that of all the Lands ſeiz'd by the Uſurpers, the Papiſts have recovered about		M. 2,340
The new Proteſtants and Churches Additions		2,400
Of a more indifferent Nature, *ut ſupra*		460
		5200
Mem. That Proteſtants in *Connaught* purchaſed of the Tranſplantees *per eſtimate.* M.		60
Wherefore of the whole 7500 M. of good Land, the *Engliſh*, and Proteſtants and Church have this *Chriſtmas* 1672.		5,140
And the *Iriſh* have near ½ as much, *viz.*		2,280
		7,500

Re-

Remains in the Common-Stock, near	80
	M.
The said 7,500 Acres of good, and the 1,500 of course, making together 9000 M. is worth *per Annum.*	M. l. 900,000
Out of which the King's Quit-rents, Old-rents, and Composition,	90,000
Rests	810,000
The Tythes whereof are one fifth, *viz.*	162,000
Rests	648,000
The benefit of Leases, and the value of Tenants Improvements upon the said Lands, is $\frac{1}{3}$ *viz.*	216,000
For the Landlords	432,000
If the whole 7500 be clearly worth but 432000 l. *per Ann.* then the 2,520 gain'd by the Rebellion, is worth but about $\frac{1}{3}$ thereof (the 80 M. in the Common Stock being worth very little), *viz.*	144,000
And the Adventurers and Soldiers Lands, who served since 1649. worth about $\frac{3}{4}$ of the same, *viz.*	108,000

And

	M.
And the ſaid Soldiers alone $\frac{3}{5}$ of the whole, *viz.*	86,400 *per An.*

Mem. That by the Succeſſes of the Army, who ſerv'd ſince 1649. and who have 85400 l. *per An.* for their labour, His Majeſty hath received the ſeveral Advantages following, *viz.*

1. Augmented the Church, the Duke of *York,* and by Proviſoes.	770 M. Acres.
2. Hath paid the Adventurers, and 49 Officers, beſides Houſing in Walled Towns	670 M. Acres.
3. Gain'd a Revenue worth above 80000 l. *per Ann.* and 15 Years Purchaſe	l. 1200,000
4. Gain'd the Years value, *&c.* worth	300,000

5. Hath freed himſelf from the 1648. Articles with the *Iriſh.*

6. Reſtored many of his Friends to their own Eſtates.

The value of the ſaid Army's Lands at ten Years Purchaſe, is 854000 l. Out of which deduct a years value and charge, there remains now but	l. 700,000 For all their Pay and Hazard.

Mem.

Mem.

That whereas until *Anno* *England* always ſent Money and other Supplies into *Ireland*, now the Revenue is 200,000 l. and the charge Civil and Military but 170,000 l. which is the gain or eaſe of *England*.

	l.
The Debentures of Commiſſion Officers, who ſerv'd eight years till about *December* 1649. comes to	1,800,000
Wherefore the Pay of private Soldiers to	5,400,000
	7,200,000

The $\frac{1}{8}$ whereof is 900,000 l. The one half whereof being for Foot, was, 450,000 l. *per Ann.* which, at 15 l. each, maintains 30,000 Foot, and the reſt 15000 Horſe, General Officers, and Train of Artillery included; ſo as there was a *Britiſh* Army, for eight Years, of at leaſt 45000 Men.

The Army who reduced the Rebellion, did *Anno* 1652, conſiſt of near 35000 Men, as *per Debentures*.

The

The *Irish* transported into Foreign parts, between 1651 and 1654. were 34,000 Men.

The *Irish* Army could not but be more than double to the *English*.

The Claymants of Land, or the number of Proprietors before the War was.

Of all that claimed innocency 7 in 8. obtained it.

The restored Persons by innocence and proviso have more than what was their own, *Anno* 1641. by at least $\frac{1}{5}$

They have gotten by forg'd Feofments of what was more than their own, at least $\frac{1}{3}$.

Of those adjudged Innocents, not $\frac{1}{20}$ were really so.

The King's Revenue in *Ireland Anno* 1641

The yearly charge of the Army for 20 years last past.

Of People, Houses, and Smoaks; their Number, Differences, and Values.

There are of People, Men, Women and Children.	1,100,000
There are of Families	200,000
Of Smoaks	250,000

VIZ.

VIZ.

Of the People, there are *English*	200,000
Of Papists	800,000
Of Non-Papists	300,000
Scots	100,000
Irish	800,000
	2,200,000

The *Scots* are *Presbyterians*, and the *Irish*, *Papists*. But the *English* are above 100,000 legal Protestants or Conformists, and the rest are Presbyterians, Independants, Anabaptists and Quakers.

Of the Families.

Such as have no fix'd Hearths, are	160,000
Such as have but one Chimney	24,000
Such as have more than one	16,000

Of Smoaks.

The Single-Smoak-houses, are *ut supra*	184,000
And those Houses that have more than one Chimney, have but one with another above four in each House, *viz.* in all	66,000
	250,M.

The

The Number of them of all degrees, who paid Poll-money, *Anno* 1661. was about	360,000
Dublin hath Houses of more than one Smoak.	3,400
Other Cities, Towns, and Corporations of the like.	6,000
The rest of *Ireland* of the like	6,600
	165,M.

And of Smiths Forges, near the same number, or rather ⅕ more.

A more particular Account of the Houses in Ireland, *which have more than one Chimney, viz.*

The Castle of *Dublin* hath Chimneys	125
The Earl of *Meath*'s House in *Dublin*	27
The Houses of *Dublin* which have above 10, are	164

The Number of Coaches, besides Hackneys, near the same Number, or rather fewer.

There be (*ut supra*) 160,000 Cabins without Chimneys, whose worth are not reckoned; but as for the others, we rate as follows, *viz.* Houses of

1 Chimney

1 Chimny	24000 at 5 *l.* each	120,000 *l.*
of 2, and 3,	6800 at 40 *l.*	272,000 *l.*
4, 5, 6,	5600 at 100 *l.*	560,000 *l.*
7, 8, 9,	2500 at 300 *l.*	750,000 *l.*
10, 11, 12,	700 at 600 *l.*	420,000 *l.*
13, 14, 15, 16, 17, 18, 19, 20.	400 at 1000 *l.*	400,000 *l.*
		2,522,000
For 20 Tranſcendental-houſes, *per eſtimate*		78,000
	Total	2,600,000

Memorandum, That not $\frac{1}{8}$ part of the Value of all thoſe Houſes do belong to other than *Engliſh* Proteſtants.	325,000
To the *Engliſh*	2,275,000
There are of Non-papiſts in *Dublin*	28,000
In the other Cities, Towns, Corporations, *&c.*	72,000
In the Country	100,000
	2,000,000

There is in Nature but one in 500 at moſt who are Blind, Lame, and under incurable Impotence; ſo as not above 2000 in *Ireland*, whom 12000 *l.* would maintain without Scandal.

The

The number of young Children under ſeven years old, and not fit for Labour, is ¼ of the whole, *viz.*	275,000
The ſaid number of Impotents	2000
The number of Soldiers	3000
	280,000

The Maſters and Miſtreſſes of 360 Families, wherein are above ſix Smoaks, are	7,200
Their Servants to their Perſons	14,400
The Servants to the Perſons of ſuch as live in 5600 Families of 4, 5, 6. Smoaks, are	11,200
Servants in Families of 2, and 3, Smoaks	6800
Miniſters, Students, &c.	400
	320,000

People in all	1100 M.
Of above 6 years old	704
16	462
26	297
36	198
46	132
56	88
66	77

So as there are in *Ireland* fit for Trade 780,000

Which

Which are Imployed as followeth, *viz.*

For the Tillage of 500,000 Acres of Land for Corn, Men, and their Wives	100,000
For Cowherds and Shepherds to Cattel, grazing upon Seven Millions of Acres, *viz.* six Millions of black Cattel, or their equivalent in Horses and Sheep. Men and their Wives.	120,000
	220,000
By the other side.	220,000
Imployed about the taking of 5000 Hogsheads of Pilchards, Boats, Nets, Hewers, *&c.* Men and Women.	1000
Imployed about making 1000 Tuns of Iron, Men and Women	2000
Smiths as by account, Men and Women	15,000
Their Servants to the Trade	7,500
Taylors and their Wives	45,000
Carpenters and Masons, and their Wives	10,000
Shoemakers and their Wives	20,000
and Servants	2500
Millers and their Wives	1600

Workers

Workers of Wooll and their Wives.	30,000
Tanners and Curriers, and their Wives.	10,000
	331,600
Trades of Fancy and Ornament and their Wives.	48,400
	380,000
Wherefore if the preſent Employment be performed with 380,000 Perſons, it follows that there are to ſpare for other uſes	400,000

Memorandum, That in *Dublin*, where are but 4000 Families, there are at one time 1180 Ale-houſes, and 91 publick Brew-houſes, *viz.* near $\frac{1}{3}$ of the whole; it ſeems, that in *Ireland*, there being 200 M. Families, that about 60 M. of them ſhould uſe the ſame Trade.

And conſequently, That 180,000 *viz.* 60 Men, 60 Women, and 60 Servants do follow the Trade of Drink.	180,000
So as there are yet to ſpare, who are Caſherers and Fait-neants.	220,000
	400,000

Whereas

Whereas it is manifest, that $\frac{2}{3}$ of the Alehouses may be spared, even although the same quantity of Drink should be sold; then there will yet be further to spare of them	120,000 and 220,000
	340,000
Having shew'd that 340,000 of spare hands are in *Ireland*, it follows to find Employments for them, which is at 7 l. *per* head, to earn *per Ann.*	2,380,000

This Implyment may be either in order to Local Wealth, or Universal Wealth.

Local Wealth I understand to be the building of 168,000 small Stone-wall Houses, with Chimneys, Doors, Windores, Gardens and Orchards, ditch'd and quicksetted; instead of the lamentable Sties now in use; the which may cost 3 l. each, in all	l. 544,000
The planting 5 Millions of Fruit-Trees at 4 d. each.	83,000
Planting 3 Millions of Timber-Trees upon the Bounds and Meers of every Denomination of Lands at 3 d. each	360,000l.

Of

	l.
Of Inclosures and Quicksets one Million of Perches at 12 d. *per* Perch.	50,000
Fortifying the City of *Dublin*	30,000
Building a new Palace for the chief Governour.	20,000
Making there a Mold for Shipping.	15,000
Making several Rivers navigable and mending High-Ways.	35·000
Building of 100 Churches, at 200 l. each	20,000
Workhouses of several sorts, Tan-Yards, Fishing Crofts, Rape-Mills, Allom and Copperas-works, as also Madder, Lead, Salt, *&c.*	50,000

In order to Money and Universal Wealth.

For Ten Thousand Tuns of Shipping	100,000
For a Stock of Wool, Hemp, Flax and Rawhides for one Years Work	400,000
For the Labour of Men to Manufacture the same.	1000,000

Of

Of the Church and Benefices.

IF $\frac{1}{5}$ the Non-Papiſts are Non-Conformiſts, then there are but 50000 Legal Proteſtants in *Dublin* and all other Cities, Towns, *&c.* which require but 50 preaching Miniſters.

And if there are but 50 M. Legal Proteſtants in the reſt of *Ireland*, they require but 100 Miniſters, at 500 to a Flock, whereof $\frac{1}{3}$, *viz.* *166* are Children.

If there be in *England* and *Wales* about 9000 Pariſhes, and under 30 Biſhops, then every Biſhop muſt have above 300 Parſons in his Charge.

So as one Biſhop in *Ireland* is more than 30 in *England*.

Wherefore 25,000 l. would afford 150 l. *per Ann.* of each of 150 Miniſters, and 2500 l. to the Biſhop

The value of the Church-Lands and appropriate Tythes, is *per Ann.* above the Kings Rent due out of them.

If 100 Miniſters can ſerve all *Ireland*, they muſt have Precincts of neer $\frac{13}{14}$ Miles ſquare, and conſequently they muſt be Itinerants, and as Lecturers on week-days; and other honeſt ordained Men muſt be Prieſts.

If

If 150, nay, if 250 Miniſters would ſerve all *Ireland*, then 10 *per Ann.* will ſupply their Mortality: And conſequently a Nurſery of 100 will ſend forth 10 yearly of 10 years ſtanding. Perhaps the Nurſery need not be above half ſo large.

Concerning the Late Rebellion.

THE number of the People being now *Anno* 1672 about 1100,000. and *Anno* 1652. about 850 M. becauſe I conceive that 80 M. of them have in 20 years encreaſed by Generation 70 M. by return of baniſhed and expelled *Engliſh*; as alſo by the acceſs of new ones, 80 M. of New *Scots*, and 20 M. of returned *Iriſh*, being all 250 M.

Now if it could be known what number of people were in *Ireland*, *Ann.* 1641. then the difference between the ſaid number, and 850, adding unto it the encreaſe by Generation, in 11 years will ſhew the deſtruction of people made by the Wars, *viz.* by the Sword, Plague, and Famine occaſioned thereby.

I find, by comparing ſuperfluous and ſpare Oxen, Sheep, Butter and Beef, that there

there was exported above $\frac{1}{3}$ more *Ann.* 1664. than in 1641. which ſhews there were $\frac{1}{3}$ more of people, *viz.* 1466,000; Out of which Sum take what were left *Ann.* 1652. there will remain 616,000. deſtroyed by the Rebellion.

Whereas the preſent proportion of the *Britiſh* is as 3 to 11; But before the Wars the proportion was leſs, *viz.* as 2 to 11. and then it follows that the number of *Britiſh* ſlain in 11 years was 112 thouſand Souls; of which I gueſs $\frac{1}{3}$ to have periſhed by War, Plague and Famine. So as it follows that 37,000 were maſſacred in the firſt year of Tumults: So as thoſe who think 154,000 were ſo deſtroyed, ought to review the grounds of their Opinion.

It follows alſo, that about 504 M. of the *Iriſh* periſhed, and were waſted by the Sword, Plague, Famine, Hardſhip and Baniſhment, between the 23 of *October* 1641. and the ſame day 1652.

Wherefore thoſe who ſay, That not $\frac{1}{8}$ of them remained at the end of the Wars, muſt alſo review their opinions; there being by this Computation near $\frac{2}{3}$ of them; which Opinion I alſo ſubmit.

There

There were transported of them into *Spain*, *Flanders*, *France*, 34,000 Soldiers; and of Boys, Women, Priests, *&c.* no less than 6000 more, where not half are returned. 40,000.

If *Ireland* had continued in peace for the said 11 years, then the 1466 M. had increased by Generation in that time to 73 M. more, making in all 1539, which were by the said Wars brought *Anno* 1652, to 850, *viz.* 689 M. for whose Blood some body should answer both to God and the King. M. 689

Anno 1650. there were before the great Plague, above one Million of People, *viz.* $2\frac{1}{3}$ more than in *London* *Anno* 1665. But in that year there died in *London* by account 97,000 people, but really were 110 M.

Wherefore, if the Plague was no hotter in *Ireland* than in *England*, there must have died in *Ireland* 275 M. But 1300 dying in a Week in *Dublin*, the Plague of *London* was but $\frac{2}{3}$ as hot; Wherefore there died in *Ireland* M. 450

So

So as ſubſtracting 412 M. 500 dying of the Plague, and 37 Maſſacred *Engliſh*, it follows that 167 M. died in 11 years by the Sword and Famine, and other Hardſhips. Which I think not incredible; for ſuppoſing ½ the Number, *viz.* 87 M. died in 11 years, of Famine and Cold, Tranſportation to *Spain* and *Barbadoes*, *&c.* it is not hard to believe, that the other 87 M. periſhed by the Sword, when the *Britiſh* had Armies of near 40 M. Men, and the *Iriſh* of near double, ſometimes on Foot.

Ann. 1653. Debentures were freely and openly ſold for 4 s. and 5 s. *per* l. And 20 s. of Debenture, one place with another, did purchaſe two Acres of Land; at which rate all the Land of *Ireland*, if it were 8 Millions of profitable Acres, might have been had for a Million of Money, which *Ann.* 1641. was worth above 8 Millions	M. 1.

The

The Cattel and Stock which *Ann.* 1641. was worth above 4 Millions, reckoning one Beef of 20 s. value, or the Equivalent in other Stock to two Acres; but *Ann.* 1652. the people of *Dublin* fetch'd Meat from *Wales*, there being none here, and the whole Cattel of *Ireland* not worth — l. 500,000

Corn was then at 50 s. *per* Barrel, which is now, and 1641. under 12.

The Houses of *Ireland*, *Ann.* 1641. was worth 2½ Millions; but *Ann.* 1652. not worth ⅕ of the same — l. 500,000

The value of people, Men, Women and Children in *England*, some have computed to be 70 l. *per* Head, one with another. But if you value the people who have been destroyed in *Ireland*, as Slaves and Negroes are usually rated, *viz.* at about 15 l. one with another; Men being sold for 25 l. and Children 5 l. each; the value of the people lost will be about — 10,355,000

The Forces kept on Foot by all Parties for the said 11 years, were at least 80,000 Horse and Foot (for even *Ann.* 1652. the *English* were 35,000 and 34,000 *Irish* transported) the Charge whereof, Train of Artillery, and General Officers included, cannot be less than 15 l. *per* Head *per Ann.* which for 11 years comes to 13 Millions and 200 M. l. — 13,200,000

The superlucration above expressed, of all which adult Men (among which were no Women nor Children) cannot be reckoned at less than 5 l. *per* Head, or $\frac{1}{3}$ of the last mentioned Sum, *viz.* — M. 4,400,000

Wherefore the effects of the Rebellion were these in pecuniary value. *viz.*

By loss of people	10,335,000
By loss of their superlucration of Soldiers	4,400,000
By the superlucration of the people lost, at 10 l. *per* Head for the whole 11 years, deducting 80 M. Soldiers	6,000,000
By impairing of the worth of Lands	11,000,000

Of

Of the Stock	3,500,000
Of the Housing	2,000,000
	37,255,000

And the 20 years Rent of all the Lands forfeited, by reason of the said Rebellion, *viz.* since the year 1652, to 1673. hath not fully defray'd the Charge of the *English* Army in *Ireland* for the said time; nor doth the said Rents at this day do the same with ½ as much more, or above 100 M. l. *per An.* more

And the Adventurers after 10 years being out of their Principal Money, which now ought to be double by its Interest, they sold their Adventures for under 10 s. *per* l. *Ann.* 1652. in open and free Market.

The Number of Landed *Irish-Papists*, or Freeholders before the Wars, was about 3000; whereof, as appears by 800 Judgments of the Court of Claims, which sate *Ann.* 1663. upon the Innocence and Effects of the *Irish*, there were not above ⅐ part or 400 guilty of the Rebellion, unto each of whom I allow 20 Followers, which would have made up an Army of 8000: But by the 49 Officers account, the *British* Army before 1649. must have been about 40 M. men; upon whom the said 8000 Nocent *Irish* so

pre-

prevail'd, as that the Peace ended in the Articles of 1648. By which the *Irish* were made at least equal Partners with His Majesty in the Government of *Ireland*; which sheweth, that the *Irish* were men of admirable Succels and Courage: Unless we should rather think, that the said Court of Claims were abused by their Perjuries and Forgeries, which one would think, that a Nation, who caus'd the destruction of so many thousand Lives, for the sake of God and Religion, should not be so guilty of.

The Estates of the *Irish* before the Wars, was double to that of the *English*; but the number and natural force of the *Irish* quintuple to that of the *English*.

The Cause of the War was a desire of the *Romists*, to recover the Church-Revenue, worth about 110 M. l. *per Ann.* and of the Common *Irish*, to get all the *Englishmens* Estates; and of the 10 or 12 Grandees of *Ireland*, to get the Empire of the whole. But upon the playing of this Game or Match upon so great odds, the *English* won and have (among, and besides other Pretences) a Gamester's Right at least to their Estates. But as for the Bloodshed in the Contest, God best knows who did occasion it.

Of

Of the future Settlement of Ireland, *Prorogation of Rebellions, and its Union with* England.

THE *English* invaded *Ireland* about 500 years since; at which time, if the *Irish* were in number about 1,200,000. *Anno* 1641. they were but 600 M. in number, 200 years ago, and not above 300,000 M. at the said time of their Invasion; for 300,000 people will, by the ordinary Course of Generation, become 1200 M. in 500 years; allowance being made for the Extraordinary Effects of Epidemical Diseases, Famines, Wars, *&c.*

There is at this Day no Monument or real Argument that, when the *Irish* were first invaded, they had any Stone-Housing at all, any Money, any Foreign Trade, nor any Learning but the Legend of the Saints, Psalters, Missals, Rituals, *&c. viz.* nor Geometry, Astronomy, Anatomy, Architecture, Enginery, Painting, Carving, nor any kind of Manufacture, nor the least use of Navigation, or the Art Military.

Sir *John Davys* hath expressed much Wit and Learning, in giving the Causes why *Ireland* was in no measure reduced to *English*

lish Government, till in Queen *Elizabeths* Reign, and since; and withal offers several means, whereby what yet remains to be done, may be still effected.

The Conquest made by the *English*, and described in the Preamble of the Act of Parliament past *Ann.* 1662. for the Settlement of *Ireland*, gave means for any thing that had been reasonable of that kind; but their Forfeiters being abroad, and suffering with His Majesty from the same usurping hands, made some diversion.

Wherefore (*Rebus sic stantibus*) what is now to be done is the Question, *viz.* What may be done by natural possibility, if Authority saw it fit?

Some furious Spirits have wished, that the *Irish* would rebel again, that they might be put to the Sword. But I declare, that motion to be not only impious and inhumane, but withal frivolous and pernicious even to them who have rashly wish'd for those occasions.

That the *Irish* will not easily rebel again, I believe from the memory of their former Successes, especially of the last, had not many Providences interpos'd; and withal from the consideration of these following Particulars, *viz.*

1. That

1. That the *Britiſh Proteſtants* and *Church* have $\frac{3}{4}$ of all the Lands; $\frac{5}{6}$ of all the Houſing; $\frac{9}{10}$ of all the Houſing in wall'd Towns, and Places of ſtrength $\frac{2}{3}$ of the Foreign Trade. That 6 of 8 of all the *Iriſh* live in a brutiſh naſty Condition, as in Cabins, with neither Chimney, Door, Stairs nor Window; feed chiefly upon Milk and Potatoes, whereby their Spirits are not diſpos'd for War. And that although there be in *Ireland* 8 *Papiſts* for 3 others; yet there are far more Soldiers, and Soldierlike-Men of this latter and leſſer Number, than of the former.

That His Majeſty, who formerly could do nothing for, and upon *Ireland*, but by the help of *England*, hath now a Revenue upon the Place, to maintain, if he pleaſes, 7000 Men in Arms, beſides a Proteſtant Militia of 25000 more, the moſt whereof are expert in War.

That the *Proteſtants* have Houſing enough within Places of ſtrength within 5 Miles of the Sea-ſide, to receive and protect, and harbour every Man, Woman and Child belonging to them, and have alſo places of ſtrength of their own properly, ſo ſituate in all parts of *Ireland*, to which they can eaſily travel the ſhorteſt day of the year.

That

That being able ſo to ſecure their Perſons, even upon all ſudden Emergencies, they can be eaſily ſupplied out of *England* with Food ſufficient to maintain them, till they have burnt 160 M. of their afore-deſcribed Cabins, not worth 50 M. l. deſtroy'd their Stacks and Haggards of Corn, and diſturbed their Tillage, which the embody'd *British* can ſoon and eaſily atchieve.

That a few Ships of War, whereof the *Iriſh* have none, nor no Skill or Practice of Navigation, can hinder their relief from all Foreign help.

That few Foreigners can help them if they would. But that none, not the King of *France*, can gain advantage by ſo doing, even tho he ſucceeded. For *England* hath conſtantly loſt theſe 500 years by their medling with *Ireland*. And at this day, than when *Ireland* was never ſo rich and ſplendid; it were the advantage of the *Engliſh* to abandon their whole Intereſt in that Countrey; and fatal to any other Nation to take it, as hath been elſewhere (as I think) demonſtrated; and the advantage of the Landlords of *England*, to give them the Equivalent of what they ſhould ſo quit out of their own Eſtates in *England*.

Laſtly,

Laſtly, Let the *Iriſh* know, That there are, ever were, and will be men diſconten-ted with their preſent Conditions in *England*, and ready for any Exploit and Change, more than are ſufficient to quell any Inſurrection they can make and abide by.

Wherefore, declining all Military means of ſetling and ſecuring *Ireland* in peace and plenty, what we offer ſhall tend to the tranſmuting one People into the other, and the thorough union of Intereſts upon natural and laſting Principles; of which I ſhall enumerate ſeveral, tho ſeemingly never ſo uncouth and extravagant.

1. If *Henry* the II. had or could have brought over all the people of *Ireland* into *England*, declining the Benefit of their Land; he had fortified, beautified and enrich'd *England*, and done real Kindneſs to the *Iriſh*. But the ſame Work is near four times as hard now to be done as then; but it might be done, even now, with advantage to all Parties.

Whereas there are now 300 M. *Britiſh*, and 800 M. *Papiſts*, whereof 600 M. live in the wretched way above mentioned: If an Exchange was made of but about 200 M. *Iriſh*, and the like number of *Britiſh* brought over

over in their rooms, then the natural ſtrength of the *Britiſh* would be equal to that of the *Iriſh*; but their Political and Artificial ſtrength three times as great; and ſo viſible, that the *Iriſh* would never ſtir upon a National or Religious Account.

3. There are among the 600 M. abovementioned of the poor *Iriſh*, not above 20 M. of unmarried marriageable Women; nor would above two thouſand *per Ann.* grow and become ſuch. Wherefore if $\frac{1}{2}$ the ſaid Women were in one year, and $\frac{1}{2}$ the next tranſported into *England*, and diſpoſed of one to each Pariſh, and as many *Engliſh* brought back and married to the *Iriſh*, as would improve their Dwelling but to an Houſe and Garden of 3 l. value, the whole Work of natural Tranſmutation and Union would in 4 or 5 years be accompliſhed.

The charge of making the exchange would not be 20,000 l. *per Ann.* which is about 6 Weeks Pay of the preſent or late Armies in *Ireland*.

If the *Iriſh* muſt have Prieſts, let the number of them, which is now between 2 and 3 thouſand Secular and Regulars, be reduced to the competent number of 1000, which is 800 Souls to the paſtorage of each Prieſt; which let be known perſons, and

English-men, if it may be. So as that when the Priests, who govern the Conscience, and the Women, who influence other powerful Appetites, shall be *English*, both of whom being in the Bosom of the Men, it must be, that no massacring of *English*, as heretofore, can happen again. Moreover, when the Language of the Children shall be *English*, and the whole Oeconomy of the Family *English*, *viz.* Diet, Apparel, *&c.* the Transmutation will be very easy and quick.

Add hereunto, That if both Kingdoms, now two, were put into one, and under one Legislative Power and Parliament, the Members whereof should be in the same proportion that the Power and Wealth of each Nation are, there would be no danger such a Parliament should do any thing to the prejudice of the *English* Interest in *Ireland*; nor could the *Irish* ever complain of Partiality, when they shall be freely and proportionably represented in all Legislatures.

The Inconveniencies of the Not-Union, and Absurdities seem to be these, viz.

1. It is absurd, that *English-men* born, sent over into *Ireland* by the Commission of

of their own King, and there sacrificing their Lives for the King's Interest, and succeeding in his Service, should therefore be accounted Aliens, Foreigners, and also Enemies, such as were the *Irish* before *Henry* the VII. time; whom, if an *English-man* had then killed, he had suffer'd nothing for it; for it is but Indulgence and Connivance, that now the same is not still in force. For such formerly was the Condition of *Irish-men*; and that of *English-men* is now the same, otherwise than as Custom has relieved them.

It is absurd, that the Inhabitants of *Ireland*, naturally and necessarily bound to obey their Sovereign, should not be permitted to know who, or what the same is, *i. e.* Whether the Parliament of *England*, or that of *Ireland*; and in what Cases the one, and in what the other. Which uncertainty is or may be made a pretence for my Disobedience.

It is absurd, that *English-men* in *Ireland*, should either be Aliens there, or else to be bound to Laws, in the making whereof they are not represented.

It is absurd if the Legislative Power be in *Ireland*, that the final judgment of Causes between man and man, should be in *England*, *viz.*

viz. the Writs of Error ſhould remove Cauſes out of *Ireland*, to the *King*'s *Bench* in *England*. That the final determination of Admiralty-Cauſes, and of ſome Cauſes-Eccleſiaſtical, ſhould be alſo ended in *England*; nor that men ſhould know whether the *Chancery* of *England* have juriſdiction in *Ireland*; and whether the Decrees of *Chancery* in one *Chancery*, can be executed in the other.

As for Inconveniences, it is one, That we ſhould do to Trade between the two Kingdoms, as the *Spaniards* in the *Weſt-Indies* do to all other Nations; for which cauſe all other Nations have war with them there.

And that a Ship trading from *Ireland* into the Iſlands of *America*, ſhould be forced to unlade the Commodities ſhipt for *Ireland* in *England*, and afterwards bring them home; thereby neceſſitating the Owners of ſuch Goods to run unneceſſary hazard and Expences.

It is inconvenient that the ſame King's Subjects ſhould pay Cuſtoms as Aliens, paſſing from one part of the ſame their own King's Territories to another.

The chief Objection againſt the remedy of theſe Evils is;

That

That his Majeſty would by the Union loſe much of his Double-Cuſtoms. Which being true, let's ſee what the ſame amounts unto; and if it be ſufficient to hinder the remedy of theſe Evils, and if it be irreparable by ſome other way.

Ann. 1664. which was the beſt year of Trade that hath been theſe many years in *Ireland*, when neither Plague nor Wars impeached it, and when men were generally diſpoſed to Splendor and Liberality, and when the Act for hindring Cattel coming out of *Ireland* into *England*, was not yet made; nor that made for unlading in *England* Ships bound from *America* into *Ireland*; I ſay, in that year the Cuſtoms upon exported and imported Commodities, between *Ireland* and *England*, was but———————————————but not $\frac{1}{8}$ thereof, which ſince, how eaſily may it be added to the other Charges upon *England* and *Ireland*, which are together perhaps 1500 M. *per Ann*?

2. If it be for the good of *England* to keep *Ireland* a diſtinct Kingdom, why do not the predominant Party in Parliament (ſuppoſe the *Weſtern* Members) make *England* beyond *Trent* another Kingdom, under Commerce, and take Tolls and Cuſtoms upon the new Borders? Or why was there

ever

ever a Union between *England* and *Wales*, the good effects and fruits whereof were never questioned? And why may not the entire Kingdom of *England* be farther Cantoniz'd, and infinitely for the advantage of Parties?

As for the Practice; The Peers of *Ireland* assembled in Parliament, may depute so many of their number, as make the $\frac{1}{8}$ part of the Peers of *England*, to be call'd by Writ into the Lords-House of *England*: And the Commons in *Ireland*, assembled in like manner, may depute the like proportion of other Members to sit with the Commons of *England*, the King and that House admitting of them.

But if the Parliament of *England* be already the Legislative Power of *Ireland*, why may they not call a competent Number out of *Ireland*, as aforesaid, or in some other more convenient manner?

All these Shifts and Expedients are necessary but for the first time, until the matter be agreed upon by both Nations, in some one Parliament.

'Tis suppos'd that the Wealth of *Ireland* is about the $\frac{1}{8}$ or $\frac{1}{10}$ of that of *England*; and the King's Revenue in both Kingdoms seems about that proportion.

Of

Of the Government of IRELAND.

THE Government of *Ireland* is by the King, 21 Biſhops (whereof four are Arch-Biſhops) and the Temporal Peers; whereof ſome part, ——-—— by reaſon of the late Rebellion, do not ſit in Parliament.

By about 3000 Freeholders, and the Members of about 100 Corporations, the Univerſity at *Dublin* reckoned for one, repreſented in the Houſe of Commons, by about 270 Knights, Citizens and Burgeſſes.

The Parliament ſo conſtituted, have a Negative upon any Law that the Lord Lieutenant and Councel ſhall offer to the King, and which the King and his Councel in *England* ſhall under the Great Seal remit to the ſaid Parliament.

The Sheriffs of Counties, and of Cities and Counties in *Ireland* are 40, finally appointed by the Lord Lieutenant, each of which hath about Ten Bailiffs.

The Chief Governour, called ſometimes Lord-Lieutenant, ſometimes Lord-Deputy, ſometimes Lords Juſtices, with a Council, at this time conſiſting of about 50 Members,

bers, do govern in all Matters belonging to the Peace, Prerogative, *&c.*

There be five Courts, *viz.* a *Chancery*, consisting of a Lord-Chancellor, Master of the Rolls, and two, three or four Sallariated Masters of *Chancery*. The *King's-Bench*, of a Lord-Chief-Justice, and two other Judges. The *Common-Pleas* of the like: The Exchequer, of a Lord-Chief-Baron, and two other Barons, with the Treasurer and Chancellor of the *Exchequer*: And a Prerogative, whereof the Primate of *Armagh* is Judge.

There is also a Palatinate-Court in *Tipperary*, whereof the Duke of *Ormond* is Lord of the Liberties and Regalities to it belonging. There is also a Court of *Admiralty*: Every Bishop hath also two Courts. And there have been formerly and lately (but now *An.* 1672. suspended) a Presidency of *Munster*, and another of *Connaght*, who meddle not with Life or Limb, nor Titles of Land.

There is also a Court-*Marshal*, for the Affairs of the Army, who in times of peace often transmit accus'd persons to the Civil-power.

To all these Courts do belong ——— ——— Officers, ——— ——— Councellors of Law, whereof I reckon ——— ——— are

of

of the first Classis, gaining by Estimation about 600 l. *per Ann.* each ———————— of the 2d. gaining about 300 l. *per Ann.* And ———————— — of the 3d gaining not above 100 l. *per Ann.* There are also ———————— sworn Attornies, gaining about 120 l. *per Ann.* one with another.

There are in *Ireland* about 950 Justices of the Peace, appointed by the Lord-Chancellor; an Head-Constable for each Barony or Hundred, being 252; and a Petty-Constable for each Parish; whereof are about 2278.

The Ecclesiastical Government is by Arch-Bishops, Bishops, Arch-Deacons, Deans of Cathedral-Churches, in all which there are now actually but one Quire entire, and that in *Dublin*, serving both at *Christ-Church*, and St. *Patrick's*. And the Parsons, Vicars and Curates for the *Protestant-Religion*, are in all *Ireland* at this day near 500, and about half the Tythes are Impropriate, and belonging to Lay-men.

This is the State of the External and Apparent Government of *Ireland*, so far as it concerns the Number and Species of Persons managing the same. But the Internal and Mystical Government of *Ireland* is thus, *viz.*

1. There

1. There are always about Twenty Gentlemen of the *Irish* Nation and *Popish-Religion*, who by reason of their Families, good Parts, Courtly Education and Carriage, are supported by the *Irish* to negotiate their Concernments at the Court of *England*, and of the Vice-Roy in *Ireland*

These men raise their Contributions by the Priests (who actually and immediately govern the People.) The Priests are govern'd by at least 24 *Romish* Bishops, all of whom have a long time been conversant in *France*, *Spain*, *Italy*, *Germany*, *England*, whereas Chaplains and Almoners, *&c.* they have made an interest with the governing Men and Ministers of State in those several Kingdoms, and have obtained some Benefits and Preferments from them.

So as the Body of the *Irish-Papists* (being about 800 M. whereof near 700 M. do live in wretched Cabbins, without Chimney or Window) are govern'd by about 1000 Secular Priests, and 2500 Friars and Regulars of several Orders; whereof most are *Franciscans*, next *Dominicans* and *Augustins*, but few *Capuchins* and *Jesuits* or *Carthusians*. These, I say, are govern'd by their respective Bishops and Superiors, whom the Ministers

nisters of Foreign States do also govern and direct.

So as upon the whole matter, the *Irish*, who are the Bulk of the Nation, are govern'd indirectly by Foreign Power; and so are the aforenamed Lay-Patriots, their support coming from the Clergy constituted as aforesaid, and who do notoriously exercise their Spiritual Jurisdiction in *Ireland*: And do also exert a Temporal Power, by prevailing with *Papist*-Justices of the Peace, to send such to Gaol as are disobedient to the Clergy, upon feigned or frivolous Complaints, which they cause to be brought against them.

The Judges aforenamed, all but the Chancellor, go Circuits, whereof there are five twice every year, excepting only the one County of *Kerry*.

There is an University at *Dublin*, but lying for the most part within one College, wherein are a Provost and seven Senior and Ruling Fellows; Nine Junior Fellows; sixty Scholars; and at this time ——— Commoners and other Students.

There was about the year 1669 erected a College of *Physicians*, consisting of a President, and 13 Fellows.

There

There are belonging to the Prerogative, Arch-Deacons Courts, Court-Martial and Admiralty-Courts, not above 10 Advocates, and 30 Proctors.

There are in the City of *Dublin* a Lord-Mayor, 2 Sheriffs, 24 Aldermen, 48 Sheriffs Peers, and 96 of the Common-Council. There are besides, Companies or Corporations of Trades-men.

There is lately instituted an Hospital for poor Children, not yet fully perfected nor endowed.

There is also an Hospital for Sick, Lame, and Old Soldiers, but without Endowment, and standing but at discretion and pleasure.

There are in and near *Dublin*, three Publick Prisons, and one House of Correction.

Lastly, I must intimate, that the Footmanship for which the *Irish* 40 years agone were very famous, is now almost quite lost among them, every man now keeping a small Garran to ride on, unless in such rocky and craggy places, where 'tis easier to go a foot than to ride.

Of the Militia and Defence of IRELAND.

THERE be in *Ireland*, as elſewhere, two Militias; one are the Juſtices of Peace, their Militia of High and Petty Conſtables; as alſo the Sheriffs Militia of his Servants and Bailiffs, and *Poſſe Comitatus* upon extraordinary occaſions.

Of theſe all together there are in *Ireland* near 3000; all of which are bound within their ſeveral Diſtricts, there to act, and not elſewhere.

There is, or hath lately been an Army in *Ireland*, of about thirty Troops of Horſe, and ſixty Companies of Foot, with a Regiment of Guard at *Dublin*, as a Life-Guard for the Lord Lieutenant, making in all about five thouſand Men.

There is alſo a Proteſtant Militia, of about 24000 Men, *viz.* about ten thouſand Horſe, and the reſt Foot.

The people of *Ireland* are all in Factions and Parties, called *Engliſh* and *Iriſh*, *Proteſtants* and *Papiſts*: Though indeed the real diſtinction is veſted and deveſted of the Land belonging to *Papiſts*, *Ann.* 1641. Of which the *Iriſh* that are veſted by Reſtoration, ſeem rather to take part with the deveſted.

sted. And the chief Pique which the *Popish-Clergy* have at the *Protestants* is, that they have the Church Livings and Jurisdictions; for the exercise of their Function they have most freely, and had, when they undertook their Project in 1641. The differences between the Old *Irish*, and Old *English Papists* is asleep now, because they have a Common Enemy.

The Old *Protestants* of Queen *Elizabeth* and King *James*'s Plantation (till of late) did not much love the New *English*; who came over since 1641. or rather since 1646. & 1648. because they envied the great Shares which they had gotten of the forfeited Lands from the Late Usurpers. But now they also are well enough together, since the said Old Protestants have had good Proviso's in the Acts of Settlement and Satisfaction for their Service before *June* 1649. and since the Church-Revenues have been augmented by the Forfeitures; but chiefly, for that the said Old *Protestants* have all the Power and Preferments Civil, Military, and Ecclesiastical.

Of the New *English*, some are *Conformists*, others not: And some have fallen in with other Parties, and others not.

Of

Of the Old Proteſtants, there are alſo Parties, I cannot] ſay Factions, chiefly denominated by the Names of their Families, as the *Butlers* and *Fitz-Gerralds* wereof old.

But to return; The chief Factions are the veſted and deveſted of forfeited Lands: all *Iriſh* and *Papiſts* generally fearing the latter, and moſt *Engliſh* and *Proteſtants* the former, as appears in all Juries and Teſtimonies given where the Lands or Lives of one or other are concerned. Now in ſome Counties, as in *Kerry*, many Forfeitures happened, and few Reſtorations, and there alſo few *Engliſh* were ever planted, nor can well endure to live: So as the firſt ſort of Militia in theſe and other like Counties, are *Iriſh-Papiſts*, deveſted and diſcontented Perſons. Whereby the few *Engliſh* there, can have no Juſtice executed, for want of hand wherewith to do it: Nor can they eaſily get indifferent Juries, but that the Sheriffs are *Engliſh* for the moſt part, and moſt commonly Proteſtants. In which Caſe, ſome have been of opinion, that the other Militia, namely the Army, may both in Law and Reaſon ſupply this defect in times when there is not occaſion for them, to guard the Land from Invaſion and Rebellion.

on. For why might not 30 Sheriffs be taken out of 120 Officers of the Army, *viz.* 60 Captains and Lieutenants of Horſe, and 60 Captains of Foot? And why may not ſuch be as reſponſible for executing juſt Sentences, as any other? And what Tenor is there in the Force which a Bailiff uſeth, more than in that which one call'd a Soldier carries with him. And why ſhould the Military Officer or Sheriff uſe more force or terror than to make the Debtor or Malefactor anſwer the Law, and obey the Sentence of a Civil Court? And is it not more convenient and eaſy in great riotous Contempts, to bring a Troop or Company, whoſe Trade it is to uſe Arms and apply Force dexterouſly, than to uſe the *Poſſe Comitatus*; that is, to call abundance of men from their Labour and Calling, to attempt things of Danger, which they do not underſtand? Moreover, if the General can quarter the Army where he pleaſes, and that the Sheriffs or Conſtable can, in their reſpective Precincts, call whom he pleaſes to his aſſiſtance; then the General can cauſe ſuch a competent Force to be quartered in thoſe thin peopled Counties. And the Sheriffs and Juſtices can call ſuch to their aſſiſtance, excepting where ſuch Soldiers are in formal

Gari-

Garisons upon actual Duty, or in other cases to be agreed upon between the Civil and Military Powers so call'd, although there can be no Countrey without Force, nor any Army without a Policy and Discipline. But of this let the Lawyers talk further.

As for the Military Force of *Ireland*, vulgarly and properly so call'd, 1. The standing Army is such as the present Revenue can well maintain, which perhaps is, or very lately was about 6000, and is every year or other year changed, as to his Majesty seems best. 2. The Protestant Militia now already established and formed, is about 24 or 25 thousand men, most of them already experienc'd in the Wars of *Ireland*.

The Third, of grand Force against Foreign Invasions, I conceive may be 70 M. Men of the best affected, and least Pope-affected *Irish*; for so many I conceive the 30000 of the standing Army and present Militia could well Officer and Command. Now that 100 M. may be spar'd to send as Soldiers in a time of extremity, I think it plain, for that there are 550 M. Males in *Ireland*, whereof 150 M. can perform all the necessary Labor of Husbandmen and Trades-men; 200 M. of them are perhaps under

der 16, and above 60. Nor doth the quality of the remaining, exempt them from service, who are to ſtand for a reſerve.

And this Force I take to be ſufficient to reſiſt any number of men which any Prince of the World hath Shipping enough to bring into *Ireland*, with ſuch Horſe, Arms, Ammunition and Victuals as are for ſuch an Enterprize.

To ſay nothing, that the ſubſtance of *Ireland* is chiefly Cattel, which be eaſily removed to waſte the Countrey where the Enemy ſhall land.

And how conſiderable the ſtanding Army of 6000 men, and the Veteran Militia, of above 24000, who have not only the Command, but the poſſeſſion and propriety of all the ſtrong and terrible Places in *Ireland*, and ¾ of all the Horſe ſerviceable in War, and at leaſt ¾ of all Shipping, and *England* to help and countenance, hath been competently mentioned before; and that the Bulk of the *Iriſh* are the Inhabitants of the aforenamed 160 M. wretched Cabins-men, ſlaviſhly bred and dealt with by their own Lords and Patriots; and that the reſtored *Iriſh*, reſtored to their Eſtates almoſt by Miracle, will be careful how they engage any more upon a frivolous, impious Undertaking

Of

Of the Cœlum *and* Solum *of* Ireland.

BY the Cœlum or Sky, I underſtand the Heat, Coldneſs, Drowth, Moiſture, Weight and Suſceptions of Air, and the Impreſſions made upon it, *viz.* The ſtate of the Winds, as whether the Wind blows in *Ireland* in compariſon with, or differently from other Places; as from what points of the Compaſs the Wind blows moſt frequently or fiercely, and what proportion of the whole year from each Point. 2. As to Heat and Cold, I conceive the ſame ought to be meaſur'd by the Weather-Glaſs or *Thermometer.* 3. As to Wetneſs or Moiſture, by the ſhrinking of Lute-ſtrings, by the quantity of Rain falling upon a certain quantity of level ſuperficies, and by the quantity of Water dried up with the ſame time out of a Veſſel of like Figure, and equal dimenſions.

As for other changes in the Air, ſuppoſed to depend upon the gravity or levity thereof, I ſuppoſe the ſame is to be known by the Inſtrument call'd the *Barrimeter. Laſtly,* To the much or little Sunſhine, whereof *Ireland* hath been much abus'd; the ſame is to be meaſur'd by an Inſtrument found for that purpoſe.

Where-

Wherefore ſince it is ſmall ſatisfaction to ſay the Air of *Ireland* is mild and temperate, inclin'd to moiſture, *&c.* And ſince the true and clear knowledge thereof depends upon ſeveral long, tedious, and reiterated Obſervations, ſimple and comparative, made in the ſeveral parts of *Ireland*, in the ſeveral Seaſons of the Year, and compar'd with the like Obſervations, made with the ſame or like Inſtruments, in the ſeveral parts of the Earth; we muſt for the preſent only ſay, that there are in being the ſeveral Inſtruments following, *viz.*

1. An Inſtrument to meaſure the motion of the Wind, and conſequently its ſtrength.

2. How many Hours in the day in the whole year it blows from any point of the Compaſs.

3. To meaſure what quantity of Rain falls in the year upon any quantity or ſpace of ground.

4. What Air is moſt deſiccative of moiſtneſs.

5. What Alterations are made in the gravity and levity of the Air from Hour to Hour.

6. The

6. The Thermometer or Weather-Glaſs of the better ſort.

7. The Inſtrument to meaſure and foretel Froſt and Snow.

Which Inſtruments many men muſt make uſe of in the ſeveral parts of *Ireland*, and the reſt of the World, and correſponding with each other, communicate and correct their Obſervation by Reaſon.

In the mean time let it ſuffice to ſay, that at *Dublin* the Wind blows 2 parts of 5 from the South-Weſt to the Weſt, one part from South-Weſt to the South; one other from the Weſt to North-Eaſt, and the reſt from the North-Eaſt to the South; 3 parts of 10 between Weſt and South-Weſt $\frac{2}{10}$ between S. W. and S. S. E. $\frac{2}{10}$ between S. S. E. and N. E. by N. $\frac{2}{10}$ N. E. by N. to N. & W. or very near thereabouts.

2. That from the 10th of *Septemb.* to the 10th of *March*, it blows a kind of Storm for ſome time or other almoſt every day.

3. That the Snow lies not long in the lower ground of *Ireland*. Nor doth it freeze more than what it doth in *France*, *Holland*, or *England*.

4. The

4. The Rain falling at *Dublin* and *London* for the Month *October*, 1663. was but 20 to 19. That the windineſs of the ſame Month was at *Dublin* 20. and at *London* but 17.

5. As for the healthfulneſs of the Climate, City, or other ſpace of Land; It muſt be firſt known how many people are in a certain day living in it, and then the *quota pars* which die *per Ann.* for many years together; and for the fruitfulneſs, how many Births.

6. As to Longævity, enquiry muſt be made into ſome good old Regiſter of (ſuppoſe) 20 perſons, who all were born and buried in the ſame Pariſh, and having caſt up the time which they all lived as one man, the Total divided by 20 is the life of each one with another; which compared with the like Obſervation in ſeveral other places, will ſhew the difference of Longævity, due allowance being made for extraordinary contingences, and Epidemical Diſeaſes happening reſpectively within the period of each Obſervation.

Wherefore Matters being not as yet prepared for theſe Experiments, I can ſay nothing clearly of them; Only, That it ſeems by the beſt Eſtimates and Approaches that I have been able to make, that *London* is more

more healthful than *Dublin* by 3 in 32.

Having said thus much of the *Cælum* or Air, or rather of the *Ingenium*, and way of distinguishing Airs in a better manner than usual: We come next to try the nature of the Soil by the like Expedients.

To which purpose, first know, that the Perch of *Ireland* is 21 Foot, that of *England* but 16 ½; Wherefore the Acre of 160 Perches is as 121 to 196, that is 121 *Irish* Acres do make 196 *English* Statute Acres. Now in *Ireland* a Milch-Cow, if *English* breed, upon two Acres of Pasture, and with as much Hay as will grow upon ½ Acre of Meadow, will yield *præter propter* 3 Gallons of Milk for 90 days, one with another, and one Gallon at a Medium for 90 more, and for 90 more scarce ¼ of a Gallon one day with another, and for 90 more, dry. Wherefore it follows, that such a Cow upon such feeding, gives above one Tun and half; nay, 384 Gallons of Milk *per Ann.* And that if the Rent of the said two Acres of Pasture be 5 s. *per Ann* and of the half Acre of Meadow 3. in all 8 s. That the Gallon of Milk comes but to a Farthing, expecting what the value and hazard of the Cow, and the labour of milking and looking to her, shall add unto that price; which I suppose not above as much more. The

The ſaid quantity of Milk will make 2½ C. of Raw-Milk-Cheeſe, and 1 C. of Whey-Butter, beſides Whey for the Swine: Or elſe 2 C. of Butter, and 1 C. of Skim-Milk-Cheeſe, beſides Whey as aboveſaid, for Drink to the People, and Food for Swine.

Mem. That one Bull ſuffices for about 20 Cows. That a Cow continues Milch and bearing, from 3 or 4 years old to 12, ſometimes 20, tho ſeldom ſuffer'd to live ſo long. And that three Dairy-women will manage 20 Cows, and do much work of other kind between while; and that one Man will look to them and their Food.

An Ox of 6 or 7 years old will not require ſo much feeding as a Milch-Cow, but will be maintained with two Acres of good Paſture only, or with 1½ Acres of Paſture, and ½ Acres of Hay, in hard Winters.

An Horſe requires 2½ Acres, as a Garran, and a ſmall Horſe or *Iriſh* Garran 1⅓, or thereabouts.

Eight or ten Sheep are equivalent for feeding to an Ox.

	l.	C.
It is further to be noted, that a Calf at a Month old weighs }		½

That

That an Ox is come to its full growth at *6* years old, and then may weigh alive } 7 C.

The 4 quarters of ſuch an Ox weighs 5 C.

The Hide, $\frac{3}{4}$

The Tallow 80 l.

And conſequently the ſaid Ox gaineth every year of weight in Fleſh to eat } l.

In Hide ——— ——

In Tallow ———

The Offal Worth, beſides half of the whole. }

The difference between lean Beef and fat Beef in value is as 5 to 9.

In Sheep the increaſe of their Fleſh, Skin and Tallow, is about the ſame proportion. And yet Sheeps Fleſh is ſold dearer than Beef, becauſe of the great trouble and hazard about Sheep.

A Fleece of Wool in *Ireland* is about 2 l. weight.

An Hog eats ſuch things as Sheep and Oxen do not, *viz.* Roots, Acorns, and conſequently the ſame Land will maintain a proportion of Hogs above Sheep and Oxen. One-Cowherd will ſerve an hundred Oxen; one Shepherd 1000 Sheep.

From

From all that hath been ſaid, we collect, that the natural and genuine Rent of Lands in *Ireland*, not that of Money, or Gold and Silver; is

Of Milk, deducting Charges —— Gall.
Of Beef and Mutton —————
Of Hides and Skin —————
Of Offall —————————
Of Wooll. —————————

So as where Lands produce more or leſs *per Ann. communibus annis* of theſe Commodities, the ſame is to be accompted more or leſs fertil than that of *Ireland*.

Moreover from hence we ſhall endeavour to gather the number of Cattel in *Ireland*, as followeth, *viz.*

There being $7\frac{1}{2}$ Millions of Acres of good Meadow, Arrable, and Paſture-Land in *Ireland*, beſides Bog with Shrub-wood, *&c.* commonly call'd unprofitable Land; and for that $\frac{1}{2}$ a Million ſupplies the Inhabitants with Corn for Bread and Drink, Man and Beaſt, Hemp, Flax and Rape, as ſhall be hereafter ſhewn from the number of the people, their manner of eating, from the number of Mills, and from the value of the Tythes, *&c.* ſuppoſing the other 7 Millions to be competently well ſtockt, let us firſt

ſee

ſee how many Houſes there may probably be.

To which purpoſe, remember that there are 184 M. Families, whoſe Houſes have but one or no Chimney. Now I gueſs, that about $\frac{1}{3}$ of this number keep a ſmall Horſe call'd a Garran, which is 61,000 Garrans for Tillage; and I ſuppoſe that the 16,000 Families have for the Coach and Saddle near 40 M. Horſes. So as in *Ireland* there are about 100 M. Horſes, whoſe Food requires 100 M. Acres of good Paſture, 50 M. Acres of Meadow, and the $\frac{1}{6}$ of an Acre of Oat-Land, *viz.* about 16,000 Acres. In all 166 M. Acres: Or if the Horſes be ſuch as require little or no Hay and Oats, as the Horſes of poor people do not, then as aforeſaid 2 or 2$\frac{1}{3}$ Acres is allowed to each Horſe.

The Wooll which is uſually exported, being a little above 2 Millions of pounds, grows upon 1000 M. Sheep: And the Wooll which cloaths the Nation, being about 1100 M. Bodies, at — l. each for Cloths, Hats and Stockins, requires 6000 M. more; and ſo 3 Millions more of Sheep, in all 4 Millions. The feeding whereof at 5 to an Acre, require 800 M. Acres. So as Horſe and Sheep require one Million of Acres. So as there remains $\frac{1}{2}$, a Million being allow'd

for

for all other Cattel, Beaſts and Vermine) $5\frac{1}{2}$ Millions for great Cattel, which will feed about 3 Millions of that Species.

If there be 3 Millions of Black Cattel, there be 1500 M. of Males, *viz.* 25 M. Bulls.	700 M. under 3 years old. 600 between 3 and 6. 175 above 6.

Of Females 1500 M. whereof $\frac{2}{5}$ are milch-Cows, *viz.* 600 M. 600 M. Calves and Heifers under 3, and 300 of other ſorts.

Where note, that of all the Black-Cattel above-named, there are 60 M. exported alive, and 30 M. dead in Barrels. Of the Sheep not 100 M.

Of Butter, whereof one of the 600 M. Milch-Cows may well yield 1 C. weight *per Ann.* but 26000 C, or the proceed of 26000 Cows. From whence may be ſeen whether the Trade of thoſe Commodities be yet at beſt: For I gueſs that the $\frac{1}{3}$ of the whole Stock may be annually ſpent at home, or exported abroad.

It remains only to ſay, that one *Iriſh* Acre of *Iriſh* Land, requires of Seed, and returns as followeth.

Seed.

Wheat 4 Buſhels, and produces 16 to 36.
Rye 4 20 to 40.

Bean-

Bean-Barly 6	20 to 48
Oats 6	16 to 32
Barley 4	20 to 40
Pease 4	12 to 18

One Horſe plows 10 Acres, and there goes 1 Man to 3 Horſes.

Of the Proportion in value, which the ſeveral Counties in Ireland *do bear to each other*, viz.

THE value or proportion of the ſeveral Counties in *Ireland*, doth ſeem much to depend upon the number of Acres which each doth contain. And therefore, and for ſeveral other Reaſons, moſt of the Land of *Ireland* hath, within theſe laſt 40 years, been admeaſured by the Chain and Inſtrument, *viz.* The King and Queens Counties, about the Year 1630. The County of *Londonderry*, when the City of *London* undertook the Plantation by one Mr. *Raven*; *Connought* and *Tipperary*, in the Earl of *Strafford*'s time, by ſeveral hands, ſometimes conducted by Mr. *William Gilbert*.

By Sir John Bodly.

The

The Lands belonging to Papists *Ann.* 1641. in the three Provinces of *Munster*, *Lemster* and *Ulster*, by Sir *William Petty.* Other Protestant Lands in the same three Provinces, in order to regulate Contributions, by the Owners of the said Lands themselves: But in so divided and separated a manner, that little Accompt can be given of them, besides what was collected by the said Sir *William Petty*; who at his own charge, besides those Maps of every Parish, which by his Agreement he delivered into the Surveyor-General's Office, he hath caused distinct Maps to be made of every Barony, or Hundred; as also of every County, engraven in Copper, and the like of every Province, and of the whole Kingdom. All which, could the Defects of them be supplied with the yet unmeasured Lands, would be exposed to publick view.

Now as to the value of these Lands, they were *Ann.* 1642. rated to and by the Adventurers as followeth, *viz.* in *Lemster* at 12 s. *per* Acre; in *Munster* at 9 s. in *Connaught* at 6 s. and in *Ulster* at 4 s. and to pay 1 Farthing *per Ann.* Quit-rent to the King out of each Shillings-worth of Land so rated, *viz.* 3 d. or 12 Farthings for an Acre in *Lemster* rated at 12 s. 9 q. or 2¼ an Acre for

for Lands in *Munster*, rated at 9 s. *& sic de cæteris.* Wood, Bog, and Mountain, to be caſt in over and above.

Afterwards the Soldiers, who were to have the ſatisfaction of their Arrears at the ſame rate, not being willing to caſt Lots upon ſuch deſperate hazards, did *Ann.* 1653. equalize Counties within each Province, *viz.* took ſome in *Lemſter*, at 1 l. 2 s. *per* Acre, ſome at 1 l. *&c.* And thoſe who were ſatisfied *Ann.* 1655. and afterwards, did equalize not only Counties, but Baronies alſo, valuing ſome Baronies in *Lemſter* at 1 l. 4 s. *per* Acre, and ſome but at 6 s. and others at all rates between theſe two extreams. But ſo as that, notwithſtanding all the ſaid differences, the whole Province ſhould be given and taken at 12 s. *per* Acre, according to the then Law. And the Inequality remaining after this Equalization, was to be corrected by a Lot.

I could here inſert all the particulars of theſe Tranſactions, but conceive it impertinent to my purpoſe, eſpecially ſince they may be ſeen upon Record. The next and beſt of all preceding equalization, was that which the Concernees of each County made in order to regulate the heavy Contributions paid to the Uſurpers before His Majeſties

jesties Restoration, and when no Quit-Rent was yet due. And in order to this work, not Baronies as before, but Parishes, nay, particular Farms were also equalized. What was done herein, was not publickly recorded, but collected by the curious, and too Bulky to be here inserted. Only take notice, that these Valuations were made as Parties interested could prevail upon and against one another by their Attendance, Friends, Eloquence and Vehemence; for what other Foundation of Truth it had in Nature, I know not.

Next to this Valuation, there was, in order to a certain Gift presented to His Majesty, by the Adventurers and Soldiers, of a years value of all their Lands as it yielded *Ann.* 1659. next immediately before his Restoration. There issued a Commission, *Ann.* 1663. to enquire and settle the said Values. And about 1667. there were made two several Valuations more; the one in order to reprize such who had restored Lands to the Innocent *Irish* in equal value; and another was a Determination what each Land was worth *Ann.* 1659. (whatever it yielded): Both which, especially the latter, are upon Record most authentically. Moreover, *Ann.* 1653, and 1654. there were Inquisitions taken of the Values which all

all and every parcel of Land in *Ireland* yielded *Ann.* 1641. There have been alſo ſeveral Acts of the chief Powers *pro tempore*, for apportioning what proportion of a certain Sum to be levied in general, ſhould in particular be charg'd on each County, *viz. Ann.* 1657. there was an Act of the Uſurper's Parliament to that purpoſe. *Ann.* 1662. There was an Act for raiſing 30 M. l. as a Preſent to his Grace the Duke of *Ormond*; and another for raiſing of for ſeveral publick Uſes. And *Ann.* 1672. for the equal raiſing of 30000 l. *per Ann.* upon all the Lands and Houſes of the whole Nation. There be alſo Accompts of what was raiſed out of each County by way of Subſidy and Pole-money, paid *Ann.* 1661. All which may be of much light to thoſe who have ſuch deſigns as the ſame will anſwer. But I being aſſur'd by whom, and for what ends, and by what means every ſuch Valuations and Inquiſitions were reſpectively made, had rather attempt ſome Rule in nature, whereby to value and proportionate the Lands of *Ireland*: The firſt whereof I propoſe to be; That how many Men, Women and Children live in any Countrey Pariſh, that the Rent of that Land is near about ſo many times 15 s. be the quantity

and

and quality of the Land what it will. 2. That in the meaneſt of the 160 M. Cabbins, one with another are five Souls, in the 24,000 ſix Souls. In all the other Houſes Ten a piece, one with another.

The TABLE.

BUT to make nearer approaches to the perfection of this Work, 'twould be expedient to know the Content of Acres of every Pariſh, and withal, what quantity of Butter, Cheeſe, Corn, and Wooll, was raiſed out of it for three years conſequent; for thence the natural Value of the Land may be known, and by the number of People living within a Market-days Journey, and the Value of their houſing, which ſhews the Quality and Expence of the ſaid People; I would hope to come to the knowledg of the Value of the ſaid Commodities, and conſequently the Value of the Land, by deducting the hire of Working-People in it. And this brings me to the moſt important Conſideration in Political Oeconomies, *viz.* how to make a *Par* and *Equation* between Lands and Labour, ſo as to expreſs the Value of any thing by either alone.

alone. To which purpose, suppose two Acres of Pasture-land inclosed, and put thereinto a wean'd Calf, which I suppose in twelve Months will become 1 *C.* heavier in eatable Flesh; then 1 *C.* weight of such Flesh, which I suppose fifty days Food, and the Interest of the Value of the Calf, is the value or years Rent of the Land. But if a Mans labour ——————— for a year can make the said Land to yield more than sixty days Food of the same, or of any other kind, then that overplus of days food is the Wages of the Man; both being expressed by the number of days food. That some Men will eat more than others, is not material, since by a days food we understand $\frac{1}{100}$ part of what 100 of all Sorts and Sizes will eat, so as to Live, Labour, and Generate. And that a days food of one sort, may require more labour to produce, than another sort, is also not material, since we understand the easiest-gotten food of the respective Countries of the World.

As for example, I suppose a pint of Oatmeal equal to half a pint of Rice, or a quart of Milk, or a pound of Bread, or a pound and quarter of Flesh, *&c.* each, in the respective place where each is the easiest

easiest gotten food. But if Rice be brought out of *India* into *Ireland*, or Oatmeal carried from *Ireland* thither; then in *India* the pint of Oatmeal must be dearer than half a pint of Rice, by the freight and hazard of Carriage, *& vice-versa, & sic de cæteris.* For, as for pleasant tast, I question whether there be any certainty, or regularity of the same in Nature, the same depending upon Novelty, opinion of Virtue, the recommendation of others, *&c.* Wherefore the days food of an adult Man, at a Medium, and not the days labour, is the common measure of Value, and seems to be as regular and constant as the value of fine Silver. For an ounce, suppose, of Silver in *Peru* is equivalent to a days food, but the same in *Russia* is equivalent to four days food, by reason of the Freight, and hazard in carrying the same from *Peru* to *Russia*; and in *Russia* the price of Silver shall grow to be worth more days labour, if a Workman can by the esteem and request of Silver Utensils earn more than he can on other materials. Wherefore I valued an *Irish* Cabbin at the number of days food, which the Maker spent in building of it.

By

By the ſame way we muſt make a Par and Equation between Art and Simple Labour; for if by ſuch Simple Labour I could dig and prepare for Seed a hundred Acres in a thouſand days; ſuppoſe then, I ſpend a hundred days in ſtudying a more compendious way, and in contriving Tools for the ſame purpoſe; but in all that hundred days dig nothing, but in the remaining nine hundred days I dig two hundred Acres of Ground; then I ſay, that the ſaid Art which coſt but one hundred days Invention is worth one Mans labour for ever; becauſe the new Art, and one Man, perform'd as much as two Men could have done without it.

By the ſame way we make an Equation between Art and Opinion. For if a Picture-maker, ſuppoſe, make Pictures at 5 *l.* each; but then, find that more Perſons would employ him at that rate than his time would extend to ſerve them in, it will certainly come to paſs that this Artiſt will conſider whether as many of thoſe who apply to him at 5 *l.* each Picture, will give 6 *l.* as will take up his whole time to accommodate; and upon this Computation he pitcheth the Rate of his Work.

By

By the ſame way alſo an Equation may be made between drudging Labour, and Favour, Acquaintance, Intereſt, Friends, Eloquence, Reputation, Power, Authority, *&c.* All which I thought not amiſs to intimate as of the ſame kind with finding an Equation between Land and Labour, all theſe not very pertinent to the Proportionation of the ſeveral Counties of *Ireland*.

Wherefore to return to the matter in hand, I ſay, that the Quantity of Commodity produced, and the Quantity of the ——— ſhews the effects of the Land; and the number of People living thereupon, with the Quality of their houſing, ſhews the Value of the Commodity; for one days delicate and exquiſit Food may be worth ten of ordinary. Now the Nature of Peoples feeding may be eſtimated by the viſible part of their Expence, which is their houſing. But ſuch helps of knowing the Value of Lands, I am not yet able to furniſh.

Of

Of the Money of IRELAND.

MOney is underſtood to be the uniform Meaſure and Rule for the Value of all Commodities. But whether in that ſence there be any Money, or ſuch Rule in the World, I know not, much leſs in *Ireland*, tho moſt are perſwaded that Gold and Silver Money is ſuch. For 1. The proportion of value between pure Gold and fine Silver, alters as the Earth and Induſtry of Men produce more of one than of the other; that is to ſay, Gold has been worth but twelve times its own weight in Silver; of late it has been worth fourteen, becauſe more Silver has been gotten. That of Gold proportionably, *i. e.* about twelve times as much Silver has been raiſed as of Gold, which makes Gold dearer. So there can be but one of the two Metals of Gold and Silver to be a fit matter for Money. Wherefore, if Silver be that one Metal fit for Money; then Gold is but a Commodity very like Money. And as things now ſtand, Silver only is the matter of Money; and that elſewhere as well as in *Ireland*.

2. The

2. The value of Silver riſes and falls it ſelf; for Men make Veſſels of coyned Silver, if they can gain by the Workmanſhip enough to defray the Deſtruction of the Coynage, and withal, more than they could expect by employing the ſame Silver as Money in a way of Trade. Now the Accidents of ſo doing, make Silver riſe and fall, and conſequently take from the perfect Aptitude for being an uniform ſteady Rule and Meaſure of all other things.

The Miſchiefs and Inconveniences hitherto mentioned, are common to all times and places; but in *Ireland* are more particular; and ſtand thus, *viz.*

A piece of 8 Rials being full 17. penny weight, paſſeth for 4 *s.* 9 *d.* if it want but $\frac{1}{2}$ a grain of the weight, tho half a grain of Silver be worth but the $\frac{1}{4}$ of a Farthing, or $\frac{1}{18}$ of a Penny, then it paſſes for 3 *d* leſs, *viz.* 4 *s.* 6 *d.* and if it weigh ten grains above 17 *d.* weight, it paſſes but for 4 *s.* 9 *d.* On the other hand, if it weigh but 12 *d.* weight, it paſſes nevertheleſs for 4 *s.* 6 *d.* And if the Silver be courſe, if not ſo courſe, as not to be called Silver, yet ſtill it paſſes for the ſame. Moreover, the fineneſs cannot be determined by common Eyes ſcarce at all, by the beſt not within 4 *d.* in an Ounce,

by

by the Touchſtone not within 2 *d.* and by the Teſt it ſelf not within an half-penny. Laſtly, The Scales and Weights differ ſo much from each other, as what is 4 *s.* 9 *d.* in one Houſe, is but 4 *s.* 6 *d.* in the next, *& vice verſa.* From whence it comes to paſs, that all pieces weighing above 17 *d.* weight, are cull'd out to buy or make pieces of 14 *d.* weight paſs for 4 *s.* 6 *d.*

2. Other Species of Coyn, which *pro rata* contain the ſame quantity of the like Gold and Silver, with the piece of eight Rials, goes in one Species for more, in another for leſs. What hath been ſaid of the Silver-ſpecies, may be ſaid of the Gold-ſpecies; and what differences are between Silver and Silver, and between Gold and Gold, is alſo between Silver and Gold Coyns. So as it becomes a Trade to ſtudy and make Advantages of theſe Irregularities, to the prejudice of the good People, who are taught, that whatever is called Money, is the ſame, and regular, and uniform, and a juſt Meaſure of all Commodities. From whence it hath happened, that all *Engliſh* Money which hath a great and deſerved Reputation in the World for its intrinſick Goodneſs, is quite carried away out of *Ireland*, and ſuch Money

ney brought instead of it, as these studied Merchants do from time to time bring in for their Advantage upon the Common People, their Credulity and Ignorance.

But Money, that is to say, Silver and Gold, do at this day much decrease in *Ireland*, for the following Reasons.

1. *Ireland*, *Anno* 1664. did not export to a much greater Value than it imported, *viz.* about 62 M. Since which time there hath been a Law made to prohibit the Importation of great Cattel and Sheep, alive or dead, into *England*; the Value whereof carried into *England* in that very year 1664. was above 150 M. *l.* The which was said to have been done, for that *Ireland* drained away the Money of *England*. Whereas in that very year *England* sent to *Ireland*, but 91 M. less than it received from thence; and yet this small difference was said to be the reason why the Rents of *England* fell $\frac{1}{5}$, that is 1600 M. in 8 Millions. Which was a strange conceit, if they consider farther, That the value of the Cattel alive or dead, which went out of *Ireland* into *England*, was but 132 M. the Hides, Tallow, and Freight whereof were worth about $\frac{1}{2}$ that Money.

2. Whereas

2. Whereas the Owners of about $\frac{1}{4}$, both of all the real and perſonal Eſtate of *Ireland*, do live in *England*, ſince the buſineſs of the ſeveral Courts of Claims was finiſhed in *December* 1668. all that belongs to them goes out, but returns not.

3. The gains of the Commiſſioners of that Court, and of the Farmers of the Revenue of *Ireland*, who live in *England*, have iſſued out of *Ireland* without returns.

4. A conſiderable part of the Army of *Ireland* hath been ſent into *England*, and yet paid out of *Ireland*.

5. To remit ſo many great Sums out of *Ireland* into *England*, when all Trade between the ſaid two Kingdoms is prohibited, muſt be very chargeable; for now the Goods which go out of *Ireland*, in order to furniſh the ſaid Sums in *England*, muſt for Example go into the *Barbados*, and there be ſold for Sugars, which brought into *England*, are ſold for Money to pay there what *Ireland* owes. Which way being ſo long, tedious and hazardous, muſt neceſſarily ſo raiſe the exchange of Money, as we have ſeen 15 *per Cent.* frequently given, *Anno* 1671. and *Anno* 1672. Altho in truth, exchange can never be naturally more

more than the Land and Water-carriage of Money between the two Kingdoms, and the enſurance of the ſame upon the way, if the Money be alike in both places.

But Men that have not had the faculty of making theſe Tranſmiſſions with dexterity, have choſe rather to give 15. *per Cent.* Exchange, as aforeſaid, than to put themſelves upon the hazard of ſuch undertakings, and the miſchief of being diſappointed.

Now the extraordinary decreaſe of Gold and Silver, put Men, whoſe Affairs were much diſturb'd, thereby upon extraordinary Conceits, and ſome very abſurd ones for Remedy, as namely the raiſing of *Spaniſh* pieces of Eight, called Cobs in *Ireland*, from 4 *s.* 9 *d.* to 5 or 6 Shillings, which were before about 5 *d.* above the Value of *Engliſh*, that is 4 *s.* 4 *d.* *Engliſh* Money weighed the ſame with a Cob called 4 *s.* 9 *d.* For theſe diſtracted People thought, that calling their Money by a better Name, did encreaſe its value.

2. They thought that no Man would carry Cobs of 5 *s.* out of *Ireland* into *England*, where they were called but 4 *s.* 4 *d.* altho he was neceſſitated to pay 4 *s.* 4 *d.* in

England,

England, and had no other effects to do it with. They thought that all Men who lived in *England*, would return to their Estates in *Ireland*, rather than pay 15. *per Cent.* for Exchange; not considering, that when Cobs were raised, that Exchange would also rise proportionably. They fancied, that he who sold a Stone of Wooll for two Cobs, call'd 9 *s.* when Cobs were rais'd, would sell his Stone of Wooll of 1 $\frac{1}{2}$ Cob when called 9 *s.* Nor did they think how this frivolous conceit would have taken away a proportionable part of all Landlords Estates in *Ireland*. As for Example, those who acted moderately, would have the Money rais'd $\frac{1}{20}$ part, and the $\frac{1}{20}$ part of all the Money of *Ireland*, was then thought to be but about 20,000 *l.* The whole Cash of *Ireland* being then estimated, but 400 M. *l.* whereas the Landlords of *Ireland*, whose Revenue is 800 M. *l. per Annum*, must have lost $\frac{1}{20}$ part of their whole Estates for ever, *viz.* 40 M. *l. per Annum* upon that empty expedient.

But others, no less sensible of the distress of the People, and the obstructions of Trade by reason of the said decay of Bullion, considering that about 600 M. *l.* would drive the Trade of that Kingdom; for that

that 300 M. would pay one half years Gale of all the Land; 50 M. would pay $\frac{1}{4}$ rent of all the Houſing, and that 150 M. would more than pay a Weeks expence of all the People of *Ireland*; and that the whole Caſh moved chiefly in thoſe Three Circles; They therefore thought to make up their 400 M. *l.* preſent Caſh by a Bank of 200 M. *l.* more, the bottom and ſupport whereof ſhou'd be Land; for the Lands and Houſes of *Ireland* being worth about 8 Millions, whereof 200 M. *l.* was but the $\frac{1}{40}$ part. 'Twas thought eaſy to find many Fortieth parts ſo free from Incumbrances or queſtion as to give a being to ſuch a Bank.

Note, that Intereſt in *Ireland* is 10 *per* Cent, which is a great hinderance to Trade; ſince the Intereſt muſt enflame the price of *Iriſh* Commodities, and conſequently give to other Nations the means of underſelling.

Of the Trade of IRELAND.

IF it be true, that there are but about 16,000 Families in *Ireland*, who have above one Chimney in their Houſes; and above

above 180 M. others; It will be easily understood what the Trade of this latter sort can be, who use few Commodities; and those such as almost every one can make and produce. That is to say, Men live in such Cottages as themselves can make in 3 or 4 Days; Eat such Food (Tobacco excepted) as they buy not from others; wear such Cloaths as the Wool of their own Sheep, spun into Yarn by themselves, doth make; their Shoes, called Brogues, are but $\frac{1}{4}$ so much worth as a Pair of *English* Shoes; nor of more than $\frac{1}{4}$ in real use and value. A Hat costs 20 *d.* a Pair of Stockins 6 *d.* but a good Shirt near 3 *s.* The Taylors work of a Doublet, Breeches and Coat, about 2 *s.* 6 *d.* In brief, the Victuals of a Man, his Wife, Three Children, and Servant, resolved into Money, may be estimated 3 *s.* 6 *d. per* Week, or 1 *d. per* Diem. The Cloaths of a Man 30 *s. per Ann.* of Children under 16, one with another 15 *s.* the House not worth 5 *s.* the Building; Fuel costs nothing but fetching. So as the whole Annual expence of such a Family, consisting of 6 in Number, seems to be but about 52 Shillings *per Ann.* each head one with another. So as 950. M. Inhabitants of these Edifices, may spend 2,375. M. *l. per Ann.* And the 150,000 who

who inhabit the 16,000 other Houſes, may ſpend 10 *l. per Ann.* each one with another, *viz.* One Million and half. So as the whole People of both ſorts ſpend under 4 Millions, whereof $\frac{1}{10}$ part, *viz.* 400 M. *l.* is for Foreign Commodities, Tobacco included, whereof every 1000 Souls ſpend one Tun *per Ann.* or every 1000 Tobacco-takers, *viz.* People above 15. Years old, ſpend two Tuns one with another: for it appears by the lateſt accompt of importance, that what is here ſaid, is true to a trifle. From whence I obſerve by the way, that the King's Revenue, *viis & modis*, being about 200 M. *l. per Ann.* that it is $\frac{1}{20}$ part of the whole Expence; which in ſome of the *Grecian* Commonwealths was thought too much, although the *Iſraelites* allowed $\frac{1}{10}$ to the *Levites* only, tho perhaps to defray the whole charge of the Government, the Supremacy amongſt that People being then Sacerdotal.

I obſerve alſo by the way, that the Lands and Houſing of *Ireland* being worth about one Million *per Ann.* that the Labour of the People may be worth three Millions, which is earned by about 750,000 (of the 1,100 M.) who by their Age and Quality are Fit and Applicable to Corporal Labours,

bours, and consequently each Labouring Person Earns but 4 *s. per Ann.* if all Work. Or if each earns 8 *l.* then but half of them work, or all but half their full time, or otherwise in other proportions. But be it one way or the other; I am as certain that the Hands of *Ireland* may Earn a Million *per Ann.* more than they now do, as I am certain that there are 750,000 in *Ireland* who could earn 2 *s.* a week, or 5 *l. per Ann.* one with another, if they had sutable employment, and were kept to their Labour.

I further observe, that if there be naturally but 2000 Impotents in *Ireland*, and that 50 Shillings *per Ann.* doth maintain the poorer sort of People; It follows, that 8,000 *l. per Ann.* would amply maintain all the Impotents of *Ireland*, if well apply'd. For other Beggers, as also Thieves, and Rebels, which are but bigger Thieves, are probably but the faults and defects of Government and Discipline.

As for the fitness of *Ireland* for Trade, we say as followeth.

1*st*. That *Ireland* consisting of above 18,000 square Miles; it is not one Place with another above 24 Miles from the Sea, because it is 750 Miles about: Wherefore forasmuch as the Land-carriage of Gross

that

that will be eaſy in ſuch a Country; it is fit for Trade, becauſe the greateſt and moſt profitable part of Trade, and the Imployment of Shipping, depends upon ſuch Goods, *viz.* Metals, Stones, Timber, Grain, Wood, Salt, *&c.*

2dly. Ireland lieth Commodiouſly for the Trade of the new *American* world; which we ſee every day to Grow and Flouriſh.

It lyeth well for ſending Butter, Cheeſe, Beef, Fiſh, to their proper Markets, which are to the Southward, and the Plantations of *America.*

Thus is *Ireland* by Nature fit for Trade, but otherwiſe very much unprepared for the ſame; for as hath been often ſaid, the Houſing thereof conſiſts of 160 M. naſty Cabbins, in which neither Butter nor Cheeſe, nôr Linnen, Yarn nor Worſted, and I think no other, can bē made to the beſt advantage; chiefly by reaſon of the Soot and Smoaks annoying the ſame; as alſo for the Narrowneſs and Naſtineſs of the Place; which cannot be kept Clean nor Safe from Beaſts and Vermin, nor from Damps and Muſty Stenches, of which all the Eggs laid or kept in thoſe Cabbins do partake. Wherefore to the advancement of Trade, the refor-

reformation of these Cabbins is necessary.

It may also be consider'd, whether the Institution of these following Corporations would not be expedient, *viz.* 1. of Cattel, 2. of Corn, 3. of Fish, 4. of Leather 5. of Wool, 6. of Linnen, 7. of Butter and Cheese, 8. of Metals and Minerals: For unto these, almost all the Commodities exportable out of *Ireland*, may be referred.

It may also be consider'd, whether the Taxing of those Cabbins with Hearth-money be proper, but rather with Days Labour; the former being scarce possible for them to have, but the latter most easy. Insomuch as 'tis more easy for them to give 40 Days Labour *per Ann.* at seasonable times, than to pay 2 *s.* in Silver at a pinch, and just when the Collectors call for it.

The Dyet, Housing and Cloathing of the 16,000 Families abovementioned, is much the same as in *England*: Nor is the *French* Elegance unknown in many of them, nor the *French* and *Latin* Tongues. The latter whereof is very frequent among the poorest *Irish*, and chiefly in *Kerry*, most remote from *Dublin*.

The

The Housing of 160 M. Families, is, as hath been often said, very wretched. But their Cloathing far better than that of the *French* Peasants, or the poor of most other Countreys; which advantage they have from their Wooll, whereof 12 Sheep furnisheth a competency to one of these Families. Which Wool, and the Cloth made of it, doth cost these poor people no less than 50 M. *l. per Ann.* for the dying it; a trade exercised by the Women of the Countrey. Madder, Allum, and Indico, are import d, but the other dying Stuffs they find nearer home, a certain Mud taken out of the Bogs serving them for Copperas, the Rind of several Trees, and Saw-dust, for Galls; as for wild and green Weeds, they find enough, as also of Rhamnus-Berries.

The Diet of these people is Milk, sweet and sower, thick and thin, which also is their Drink in Summer-time, in Winter Small-Beer or Water. But Tobacco taken in short Pipes seldom burnt, seems the pleasure of their Lives, together with Sneezing: Insomuch, that $\frac{2}{7}$ of their Expence in Food, is Tobacco. Their Food is Bread in Cakes, whereof a Penny serves a Week for each; Potatoes from *August* till *May*, Muscles, Cockles and Oysters, near the Sea; Eggs

Eggs and Butter made very ra cid, by keeping in Bogs. As for Flesh, they seldom eat it, notwithstanding the great plenty thereof, unless it be of the smaller Animals, because it is inconvenient for one of these Families to kill a Beef, which they have no convenience to save. So as 'tis easier for them to have a Hen or Rabbet, than a piece of Beef of equal substance.

Their Fewel is Turf in most places; and of late, even where Wood is most plentiful, and to be had for nothing, the cutting and carriage of the Turf being more easy than that of Wood. But to return from whence I digressed, I may say, That the Trade of *Ireland*, among $\frac{19}{22}$ parts of the whole people, is little or nothing, excepting for the Tobacco abovementioned, estimated worth about 50,000 l. for as much as they do not need any Forreign Commodities, nor scarce any thing made out of their own Village. Nor is above $\frac{1}{5}$ part of their Expence other than what their own Family produceth, which Condition and state of living cannot beget Trade.

And now I shall digress again to consider, whether it were better for the Commonwealth to restrain the expence of 150 M. *Optimates* below 10 l. *per Ann.* each; or to to beget a luxury in the 950 M. Plebeians, ſo as to make them ſpend, and conſequently earn double to what they at preſent do.

To which I anſwer in brief, That the one ſhall encreaſe the ſordidneſs and ſqualor of living already too viſible in 950 M. Plebeians, with little benefit to the Common Wealth; the other ſhall increaſe the ſplendor, Art and Induſtry of the 950 M. to the great enrichment of the Common-Wealth.

Again, Why ſhould we be forbid the uſe of any Foreign Commodity, which our own Hands and Countrey cannot produce, when we can employ our ſpare Hands and Lands upon ſuch exportable Commodities as will purchaſe the ſame, and more.

3. The keeping or leſſening of money, is not of that conſequence that many gueſs it to be of. For in moſt places, eſpecially *Ireland*, nay, *England* it ſelf, the Money of the whole Nation is but about $\frac{1}{10}$ of the Expence of one Year; *viz.* *Ireland* is thought to have about 400 M. l in Caſh, and to ſpend about 4 millions *per Ann.* Wherefore it is very ill-husbandry to double the Caſh of the Nation, by deſtroying half its Wealth; Or to increaſe the Caſh otherwiſe than

than by increaſing the Wealth *ſimul & ſemel.*

That is, when the Nation hath $\frac{1}{10}$ more Caſh, I require it ſhould have $\frac{1}{10}$ more Wealth, if it be poſſible. For, there may be as well too much money in a Country, as too little. I mean, as to the beſt advantage of its Trade; onely the Remedy is very eaſy, it may be ſoon turn'd into the magnificence of Gold and Silver Veſſels.

Laſtly, Many think that *Ireland* is much impoveriſhed, or at leaſt the money thereof much exhauſted, by reaſon of Abſentees, who are ſuch as having Lands in *Ireland*, do live out of the Kingdom, and do therefore think it juſt that ſuch, according to former Statutes, ſhould loſe their ſaid Eſtates.

Which Opinion I oppoſe, as both unjuſt, inconvenient, and frivolous. For 1ſt. If a man carry Money or other Effects out of *England* to purchaſe Lands in *Ireland*, why ſhould not the Rents, Iſſues and Profits of the ſame Land return into *England*, with the ſame Reaſon that the Money of *England* was diminiſhed to buy it?

2. I ſuppoſe $\frac{1}{4}$ of the Land of *Ireland* did belong to the Inhabitants of *England*, and that the ſame lay all in one place together; why may not the ſaid quarter of the

whole

whole Land be cut off from the other three ſent into *England*, were it poſſible ſo to do? and if ſo, why may not the Rents of the ſame be actually ſent, without prejudice to the other three parts of the Intereſſors thereof?

3. If all men were bound to ſpend the Proceed of their Lands upon the Land it ſelf; then as all the Proceed of *Ireland*, ought to be ſpent in *Ireland*; ſo all the Proceed of one County of *Ireland*, ought to be ſpent in the ſame; of one Barony, in the ſame Barony; and ſo Pariſh and Mannor; and at length it would follow, that every eater ought to avoid what he hath eaten upon the ſame Turf where the ſame grew. Moreover, this equal ſpreading of Wealth would deſtroy all Splendor and Ornament; for if it were not fit that one place ſhould be more ſplendid than another, ſo alſo that no one man ſhould be greater or richer than another; for if ſo, then the Wealth, ſuppoſe of *Ireland*, being perhaps 11 Millions, being divided among 1,100 M. people, then no one man having above 10 l. he could Probably build no Houſe worth above 3 l. which would be to leave the face of Beggery upon the whole Nation: And withal ſuch Parity would beget Anarchy and Confuſion.

Of

Of the other Impediment of Trade, the not raiſing of Money above the value which the generality of the whole World hath of it, that is, the intrinſick value, I have ſpoken before: And now return to other matters relating to the Trade of *Ireland.*

Having ſhewn that there is little or no Trade or Commutation of Commodities, where people live ſo ſimply, and as it were *ex ſponte creatis*, as the Inhabitants of 184 M. do live; It follows, that what Trade is in *Ireland* muſt be found in the 16,000 other Houſes of above one Chimney in each, and amongſt the Inhabitants of them. Though Trade, properly ſpeaking, be the Commutation of Commodities; that generally ſpeaking, 'tis the way whereby to purchaſe Riches and Power, the Parents of Pleaſure: Not only by getting Commodities out of the Earth and Sea; by ploughing, fiſhing, Mines, Vecture, &c. by getting away thoſe Commodities from them, who firſt got them out of the Earth and Sea, as aforeſaid. And not only, or at all encreaſing the whole Wealth of the Nation, but ones own former ſhare and proportion of the whole, though diminiſh'd; that is to ſay, Suppoſing the whole Wealth of *Ireland* were 10 Millions, and the Share of of A. was 1000 l. thereof; I ſay, 'tis commonly more the care of A. to make his 1000 l. 3000, though by leſſening the whole Stock 2000 l. than to make the whole Stock 30 Millions, by leſſening his own 1000 l. to 300. l.

Now this is the Trade of *Ireland*, and I think of moſt other places, but exerciſed in *Ireland* by the following ways, *viz.*

Whereas the Lands of *Ireland* have within 150 years been moſt of them forfeited, and the Lands of Monaſteries have ſince then fallen into the King's hands, by the diſſolution of the ſaid Monaſteries, and ſeveral Defects found in the Titles, older than that of time; It hath come to paſs, that all the ſaid Lands have been granted to ſeveral others; ſome legally and formally, ſome otherwiſe; ſome under one Condition, ſome under another. So as by ſeveral Defects in the ſaid Grants, or by non-performance of Conditions, and many other ways needleſs to enumerate, the King in ſtrictneſs may find a Title to the Eſtates of many men who have been long in poſſeſſion of their reſpective Holdings, (tho ſome more, ſome leſs, ſome upon better, and ſome upon worſer grounds.) A principal Trade in *Ireland*, to find out theſe

Flaws

Flaws and Defects, to procure Commiſſion for ſuch Inquiries. And a Branch of this Trade, is to give to ſuch ſeekers flattering and deluſive Informations to bring on other Deſigns ; and withal, prevail with perſons converſant with the Higher Powers, to give Grants of theſe Diſcoveries, and thereupon, right or wrong to vex the Poſſeſſors, at leaſt into ſuch a Compoſition, as may be of profit to the Proſecutors. Whereby it falls out, that the time of all the perſons exerciſed *pro & contra* in theſe matters, who do only take from one another like Gameſters (the Lawyers taking from both) is loſt, without advancing at all the Publick Wealth. Now this is no Trade, but a Calamity upon the Nation.

2. Whereas the Branches of the Publick Revenue being manifold, and the Accompts of the ſame vaſt and numerous, and the Laws, with the Caſes and Accidents relating to the ſame, intricate and new ; but chiefly the Officers employed about the Premiſes, ſuch as could make Friends for their Places, whether Perſons of Skill, Experience and Truſtineſs, or not ; It hath come to paſs, even in *Ireland*, in former times, that Principal Officers of the Exchequer have repreſented the State of the Publick Treaſury

Treaſury near 200M.l.differently from each other : So as new men have been admitted totake the whole to farm,who expected vaſt Advantages, by mending and clearingwhat others had marr'd and confounded, though they had ſtill their Places and Perquiſites notwithſtanding: And in this caſe the people thought fit to pay any thing that was required,rather than to paſs theFire of thisPurgatory,even tho they need no burning.

This and other Practices of Farming, taken with the whole Doctrine of Defalcations, hath been a great Trade in *Ireland*, but a Calamity on the people who have paid great Wages to them that have made Faults, but three times greater to thoſe who would but undertake to mend them, tho indeed they could not.

A Third great Trade and Calamity to the people of *Ireland*, hath been the Gains made by the aforementioned Difference, Confuſion, and badneſs of Coins, exorbitant Exchange, and Intereſt of Money, all following alſo from the Premiſes.

A Fourth Calamity is implicating poor Work-men, and trapanning them into Crimes, Indictments, Biſhops-Courts, *&c.* feigning and compounding of Treſpaſſes, not without making benefit by the Office of Juſtice of Peace.

A Fifth may be from the manner of making Sheriffs, the execution of their Offices, Accompts in the Exchequer, *&c.*

A Sixth, from raiſing Moneys at the Aſſizes, by Authority of the Grand Juries, but raiſing too much, and in ſpending or not ſpending what was to be raiſed.

None of theſe Six Trades do add any more to the Common-wealth than Gameſters, and even ſuch of them as play with falſe Dice, do to the Common-Stock of the whole Number.

And in theſe Trades 'tis thought; of thoſe who inhabit the aforementioned 16,000 Houſes, do exerciſe themſelves, and are the Locuſts and Catterpillars of the Common-wealth, as the Inhabitants of the other 184 M. Cottages are the untilled part of the ſame. Wherefore it remains to ſee what Trade is to be found among the reſt; which I take to be as followeth, *viz.*

1. In Domeſtick-Wealth: Of which ſort is building fine Houſes and Gardens, Orchards, Groves, Inns, Mills, Churches, Bridges, HighWays, Cauſeys; as alſo Furniture for Houſes, Coaches, *&c.* In which kind I gueſs the Improvement of *Ireland* has ſince the Year 1652. 1673. advanc'd from

from one to four, and I think to a better ſtate than before 1641. that is, than perhaps ever it yet was.

The Foreign Trade, if you will believe the Accompts of Cuſtoms, *Ann.* 1657. and now, hath been advanced from one to ſeven, but in reality, I think, from one to two: For the Cuſtoms yielded *Ann.* 1656. clear under 12,000 *l.* but were within a year or two, let for above three times the ſum, but are now at about 80,000 intrinſecally.

But to ſpeak more clearly and Authentically upon this Subject, I ſhall inſert the following Tables of exported and imported Commodities, and from them make the ſubnexed Obſervations, *viz.*

The TABLES.

1. THAT the Cuſtoms, managed by the States-Officers, yielded *Anno* 1657. under 12,000 *l.* but was farm'd *Ann.* 1658. for above thrice that Sum.

2. That the Stock which drives the Foreign Trade of *Ireland*, doth near half of

of it belong to those who live out of *Ireland.*

3. That *Ann.* 1664. before the Cattel-Statute, $\frac{3}{4}$ of the *Ireland* Foreign Trade was with *England*, but now not $\frac{1}{4}$ part of the same.

4. That the Manufacture bestowed upon a years Exportation out of *Ireland*, is not worth above 8000 *l.*

5. That because more eatables were exported *Anno* 1664. than 1641. And more Manufactures 1641. than *Ann.* 1664. It follows, there were more people in *Ireland*, *Ann.* 1641. than 1664. and in that proportion as was formerly mention'd.

6. That the Exportations appear more worth than the Importations, excepting that the Accompts of the former are more true, but of the latter very conjectural, and probably less than the Truth.

Of

Of the Religion, Diet, Cloaths, Language, Manners, and Intereſt of the ſeveral preſent Inhabitants of IRELAND.

WE ſaid, that of the 1100 M. Inhabitants of *Ireland*, about 800 M. of them were *Iriſh*; and that above 600 M. of them lived very ſimply in the Cabbins aforemention'd. Wherefore I ſhall in the firſt place deſcribe the Religion, Diet, *&c.* of theſe, being the major part of the whole; not wholly omitting ſome of the other ſpecies alſo.

The Religion of theſe poorer *Iriſh*, is called *Roman Catholick*, whoſe Head is the Pope of *Rome*, from whence they are properly enough called *Papiſts*. This Religion is well known in the World, both by the Books of their Divines, and the Worſhip in their Churches: wherefore I confine my ſelf to what I think peculiar to theſe *Iriſh*. And firſt, I obſerve, that the Prieſts among them are of ſmall Learning; but are thought by their Flocks to have much, becauſe they can ſpeak Latin more or leſs; and can often out-talk in Latin thoſe who Diſpute with them. So as they are thereby

thereby thought both more Orthodox and Able than their Antagonists.

Their Reading in Latin is the Lives of the Saints, and Fabulous Stories of their Country. But the Superior Learning among them, is the Philosophy of the Schools, and the Genealogies of their Ancestors. Both which look like what St. *Paul* hath Condemned.

The Priests are chosen for the most part out of old *Irish* Gentry; and thereby influence the People, as well by their Interest as their Office.

Their Preaching seems rather Bugbearing of their flocks with dreadful Stories, than persuading them by Reason, or the Scriptures. They have an incredible Opinion of the Pope and his Sanctity, of the happiness of those who can obtain his Blessing at the third or fourth hand. Only some few, who have lately been abroad, have gotten so far, as to talk of a difference between the Interest of the Court of *Rome*, and the Doctrine of the Church. The Common Priests have few of them been out of *Ireland*; and those who have, were bred in Covents, or made Friars for the most part, and have humble Opinions of the *English* and Protestants, and of the mischiefs

chiefs of ſetting up Manufactures, and introducing of Trade. They alſo comfort their Flocks, partly by Prophecies of their Reſtoration to their Ancient Eſtates and Liberties, which the abler ſort of them fetch from what the Prophets of the Old-Teſtament have delivered by way of God's Promiſe to reſtore the *Jews*, and the Kingdom to *Iſrael*. They make little eſteem of an Oath upon a Proteſtant Bible, but will more devoutly take up a Stone, and ſwear upon *it*, calling it a Book, than by the ſaid Book of Books, the Bible. But of all Oaths, they think themſelves at much liberty to take a Land-Oath, as they call it: Which is an Oath to prove a forg'd Deed, a Poſſeſſion, Livery or Seiſin, payment of Rents, *&c.* in order to recover for their Countrey-men the Lands which they had forfeited. They have a great Opinion of Holy-Wells, Rocks, and Caves, which have been the reputed Cells and Receptacles of men reputed Saints, They do not much fear Death, if it be upon a Tree, unto which, or the Gallows, they will go upon their Knees toward it, from the place they can firſt ſee it. They confeſs nothing at their Executions, though never ſo guilty. In brief, there is much Superſtition among them, but formerly much more

more than is now; for as much as by the Converſation of Proteſtants, they become aſham'd of their ridiculous Practices, which are not *de fide*. As for the Richer and better-educated ſort of them, they are ſuch Catholicks as are in other places. The Poor, in adhering to their Religion, which is rather a Cuſtom than a Dogma amongſt them, They ſeem rather to obey their Grandees, old Landlords, and the Heads of their Septes and Clans, than God. For when theſe were under Clouds, tranſported into *Spain*, and tranſplanted into *Connaught*, and diſabled to ſerve them as formerly, about the year 1656. when the Adventurers and Soldiers appeared to be their Landlords and Patrons, they were obſerv'd to have been forward enough to relax the ſtiffneſs of their pertinacity to the Pope, and his Impoſitions. *Laſtly*, Among the better ſort of them, many think leſs of the Pope's Power in Temporals, as they call it, than formerly; and begin to ſay, that the Supremacy, even in Spirituals, lies rather in the Church diffuſive, and in qualified General-Councils, than in the Pope alone, or than in the Pope and his Cardinals, or other *Juncto*.

The Religion of the Proteſtants in *Ireland*, is the ſame with the Church of *Eng-*

lands

land in Doctrine, only they differ in Discipline thus, *viz.*

The Legal Proteſtants hold the Power of the Church to be in the King, and that Biſhops and Arch-Biſhops, with their Clerks, are the beſt way of adjuſting that Power under him. The Presbyterians would have the ſame thing done, and perhaps more, by Claſſes of Presbyters National and Provincial. The Independents would have all Chriſtian Congregations independent from each other. The *Anabaptiſts* are Independent in Diſcipline, and differ from all thoſe aforemention'd in the Baptiſm of Infants, and in the inward and ſpiritual Signification of that Ordinance. The Quakers ſalute not by uncovering the Head, ſpeak to one another in the ſecond Perſon, and ſingular Number; as for Magiſtracy and Arms, they ſeem to hold with the *Anabaptiſts* of *Germany* and *Holland*; they pretend to a poſſibility of perfection, like the Papiſts; as fo. other Tenents, 'tis hard to fix them, or to underſtand what things they mean by their Words.

The Diet of the poorer *Iriſh*, is what was before diſcourſed in the Chapter.

The

The Cloathing is a narrow ſort of Frieze, of about twenty Inches broad, whereof two foot, call'd a Bandle, is worth from $3\frac{1}{2}$ to 18 *d.* Of this, Seventeen Bandles make a Man's Suit, and twelve make a Cloak. According to which Meaſures and Proportions, and the number of People who wear this Stuff, it ſeems, that near thrice as much Wooll is ſpent in *Ireland*, as exported; whereas others have thought quite contrary, that is, that the exported Wooll is triple in quantity to what is ſpent at home.

As for the Manners of the *Iriſh*, I deduce them from their Original Conſtitutions of Body, and from the Air; next from their ordinary Food; next from their Condition of Eſtate and Liberty, and from the Influence of their Governours and Teachers; and laſtly, from their Ancient Cuſtoms, which affect as well their Conſciences as their Nature. For their Shape, Stature, Colour, and Complexion, I ſee nothing in them inferior to any other People, nor any enormous predominancy of any humour.

Their Lazing ſeems to me to proceed rather from want of Imployment and Encouragement to Work, than from the natural

tural abundance of Flegm in their Bowels and Blood; for what need they to Work, who can content themſelves with *Potato's*, whereof the Labour of one Man can feed forty; and with Milk, whereof one Cow will, in Summer time, give meat and drink enough for three Men, when they can every where gather Cockles, Oyſters, Muſcles, Crabs, *&c.* with Boats, Nets, Angles, or the Art of Fiſhing; can build an Houſe in three days? And why ſhould they deſire to fare better, tho with more Labour, when they are taught, that this way of living is more like the Patriarchs of old, and the Saints of later times, by whoſe Prayers and Merits they are to be reliev'd, and whoſe Examples they are therefore to follow? And why ſhould they breed more Cattel, ſince 'tis Penal to import them into *England?* Why ſhould they raiſe more Commodities, ſince there are not Merchants ſufficiently Stock'd to take them of them, nor provided with other more pleaſing foreign Commodities, to give in Exchange for them? And how ſhould Merchants have Stock, ſince Trade is prohibited and fetter'd by the Statutes of *England?* And why ſhould Men endeavour to get Eſtates, where the Legiſlative Power is not agreed upon; and where

where Tricks and Words deſtroy natural Right and Property?

They are accuſed alſo of much Treachery, Falſeneſs, and Thievery; none of all which, I conceive, is natural to them; for as to Treachery, they are made believe, that they all ſhall flouriſh again, after ſome time; wherefore they will not really ſubmit to thoſe whom they hope to have their Servants; nor will they declare ſo much, but ſay the contrary, for their preſent eaſe, which is all the Treachery I have obſerved; for they have in their hearts, not only a grudging to ſee their old Proprieties enjoyed by Foreigners, but a perſuaſion they ſhall be ſhortly reſtor'd. As for Thievery, it is affixt to all thin-peopled Countries, ſuch as *Ireland* is, where there cannot be many Eyes to prevent ſuch Crimes; and where what is ſtolen, is eaſily hidden and eaten, and where 'tis eaſy to burn the Houſe, or violate the Perſons of thoſe who proſecute theſe Crimes, and where thin-peopled Countries are govern'd by the Laws that were made and firſt fitted to thick-peopled Countries; and where matter of ſmall moment and value muſt be try'd, with all the formalities which belong to the higheſt Cauſes. In this caſe there

muſt

muſt be thieving, where is withal, neither encouragement, nor method, nor means for Labouring, nor Proviſion for Impotents.

As for the Intereſt of theſe poorer *Iriſh*, it is manifeſtly to be tranſmuted into *Engliſh*, ſo to reform and qualify their houſing, as that *Engliſh* Women may be content to be their Wives, to decline their Language, which continues a ſenſible diſtinction, being not now neceſſary; which makes thoſe who do not underſtand it, ſuſpect, that what is ſpoken in it, is to their prejudice. It is their Intereſt to deal with the *Engliſh*, for Leaſes, for Time, and upon clear Conditions, which being perform'd they are abſolute Freemen, rather than to ſtand always liable to the humour and caprice of their Landlords, and to have every thing taken from them, which he pleaſes to fancy. It is their Intereſt, that he is well-pleaſed with their Obedience to them, when they ſee and know upon whoſe Care and Conduct their well-being depends, who have Power over their Lands and Eſtates. Then, to believe a Man at *Rome* has Power in all theſe laſt mentioned Particulars in this World, and can make them eternally happy or miſerable hereafter, 'tis their

their Intereſt to joyn with them, and follow their Example, who have brought Arts, Civility, and Freedom into their Country.

On the contrary, What did they ever get by accompanying their Lords into Rebellion againſt the *Engliſh*? What ſhould they have gotten if the late Rebellion had abſolutely ſucceeded, but a more abſolute Servitude? And when it fail'd, theſe poor People have loſt all their Eſtates, and their Leaders encreas'd theirs, and enjoy'd the very Land which their Leaders caus'd them to loſe. The pooreſt now in *Ireland* ride on Horſe-back, when heretofore the beſt ran on foot like Animals. They wear better Cloaths than ever; the Gentry have better Breeding, and the generality of the *Plebeians* more Money and Freedom.

Several Miſcellany Remarks and Intimations, concerning Ireland, *and the ſeveral Matters aforementioned.*

WIthout recourſe to the Authority of Story, but rather diligently obſerving the Law and Courſe of Nature, I conjecture, that whatever is fabled of the *Phœnicians*, *Scythians*, *Biſcayers*, *&c.* their firſt Inhabiting of *Ireland*; that the places near *Carrickfergus* were firſt peopled, and that with thoſe, who came from the parts of *Scotland* oppoſite thereunto. For that *Ireland* was planted by ſome body in *Caſar*'s time, is moſt certain. That the Art of Navigation was not before *Caſar*'s time ſo well underſtood and practis'd, as to bring Men from any other Part of the World thither, ſave from *Great Britain*: That from St. *Davids-head* in *South-Wales*, and from *Holy-head* in *North-Wales*, *Ireland* is not clearly at any time diſcern'd, nor often at all. That the Inhabitants of thoſe two *Brittiſh* Head-lands had neither Boats fit to paſs that Sea, is moſt probable. But that *Carrickfergus* may be always ſeen from *Scotland*, is well known; and that a ſmall

Boat

Boat may Row over in three or four hours, is experienc'd. That the Language of those Parts differ very little. That the Country about *Carrickfergus* is far better than that of *Scotland* opposite. That the chief Bishops Seat of *Ireland*, and probably the first, is near those Parts, are all notorious Truths. From all which 'tis more probable, that *Ireland* was first Peopled from *Scotland*, than all the other remote Parts aforementioned.

It hath been much observed, That the Lieutenants and Chancellors of *Ireland* have often been at variance; the reason whereof seems to be at their Powers, and too near an *Equilibrium*; for the Lieutenant Commands an Army perhaps of 3000, and the Chancellor makes 900 Justices of Peace, who make 2500 Constables, which are the Civil Sword, who Act in times of Peace, and every where, and in all matters; whereas the Army acts only upon rare occasions, and are more Mercenary Men. So as the Civil-Sword seems of far more extent and effect than the Military-Sword.

The Lieutenant disposes perhaps of four or five hundred Places and Imployments; but the Chancellor, of the said nine hundred Justices

Justices of Peace, and several others. The Lieutenant can hurt very few Persons, who do not depend upon the favour of Imployments; but the Chancellor can affect all Men, of Estates and Dealing in the World, by the Power of his Court, and by the Harmony of his own Will with the King's Conscience.

The Lieutenant is for the most part a Stranger to *Ireland*; but the Chancellor seldom such, but a Person of great Family and Acquaintance. Moreover, all the Lieutenants, Deputies, and Lords Justices, that have been these 150 years, have not, one with another, continued two years in the Office; but the Chancellors have much more, and are seldom remov'd but by Death, and General Revolutions. The Chancellor has ordinarily some other Dignity and Office annex'd, for they be often Eminent Prelates and Church-men; but the Lieutenant is confin'd to Temporals. The Chancellor is Speaker in Parliament, and by keeping the Seal, can check the Lieutenant in many cases. The Chancellors are bred to Eloquence and Arguing; the breeding of a Lieutenant is casual.

Men

Men that bring great Eſtates into *Ireland*, do not encreaſe them proportionably with them who come over with nothing. Not to quote the Examples hereof on both ſides, the reaſon ſeems not to be very abſtruſe, *viz.*

The Language of *Ireland* is like that of the *North* of *Scotland*, in many things like the *Welch* and *Manques*; but in *Ireland* the *Fingallians* ſpeak neither *Engliſh*, *Iriſh*, nor *Welch*; and the People about *Wexford*, tho they agree in a Language differing from *Engliſh*, *Welch*, and *Iriſh*, yet 'tis not the ſame with that of the *Fingalians* near *Dublin*. Both theſe two ſorts of People are honeſt and laborious Members of the *Kingdom*.

The *Iriſh* Language, and the *Welch*, as alſo all Languages that have not been the Languages of flouriſhing Empires, wherein were many Things, many Notions and Fancies, both Poetical and Philoſophical, hath but few words; and all the names of Artificial things brought into uſe, ſince the Empire of theſe Linguiſts ceaſed, are expreſſed in the language of their Conquerors, by altering the Termination and Accents only.

Ireland

Ireland is now divided into Provinces, Counties, Baronies, Pariſhes, and Farm-lands, and thoſe, ſo as that they may be, and have been Geometrically delineated; but formerly it was not ſo, but the Country was called by the names of the Lords who governed the People. For as a Territory bounded by Bogs, is greater or leſſer as the Bog is more dry and paſſible, or otherwiſe: So the Country of a Grandee or Tierne in *Ireland*, became greater or leſſer as his Forces waxed or weaned; for where was a large Caſtle and Gariſon, there the Juriſdiction was alſo large.

And when theſe Grandees came to make peace, and parts one with another, the limits of their Land-agreements were no lines Geometrically drawn; but if the Rain fell one way, then the Land whereon it fell, did belong to A, if the other way, to B. *&c.*

As to their Town-lands, Plough-lands, Colps, Gneeres, Bullibos, Ballibelaghs, Two's, Horſmens, Beds, *&c.* they are all at this day become unequal both in Quantity and Value, having been made upon grounds which are now Obſolete and Antiquated.

For

For ſometimes lands were divided by what certain Societies of men held, which I conceive were Town-lands or Tythings.

Sometimes by Plow-lands, viz. ſuch a ———— of Lands as contained enough of every ſpecies of Land Arrable, Meadow, and Paſture, Mountain, Turf-bog, Wood, *&c.* as ſerv'd for the whole Uſe of man, eſpecially of the Owner of ſuch a Plow-land.

Sometimes by the Share or Proportion of Land, which an Undertaker would engage to plant and defend according to Articles.

Sometimes by the Share which each Servitor had given him in reward for his Service, after a Rebellion or Inſurrection.

Sometimes by what belonged to the Cell of ſome Religious Man or Men. But now all the Lands are Geometrically divided, and that without aboliſhing the Ancient Denominations and Diviſions abovementioned. So that it is yet wanting to prevent the various ſpelling of Names not underſtood, that ſome both comprehending the Names of all publick Denominations according as they are ſpelled in the lateſt Grants, ſhould be ſet out by Authority to determine the ſame

ſame for the time to come. And that where the ſame Land hath other Names, or hath been ſpelled with other Conſcription of Letters or Syllables,that the ſame be mentioned with an *alias*. Where the publick and new authenticated Denominations is part of a greater antiquated Denomination, that it be ſo expreſſed, as by being called the *Eaſt*, *Weſt*, *South* or *North* part thereof. And if the ſaid Denomination comprehend ſeveral obſolete or inconſiderable Parcels, that the ſame be expreſſed likewiſe.

The laſt Clauſe of the Explanatory Act, enabled men to put new Names on their reſpective Lands, inſtead of thoſe uncouth, unintelligible ones yet upon them. And it would not be amiſs if the ſignificant part of the *Iriſh* Names were interpreted, where they are not, or cannot be aboliſhed.

Some

SOME have thought that little Shipping belongs to *Ireland*, by the great Policy of the *English*, who (as they wittily expressed it) would keep the Chain or Draw-Bridge between both Kingdoms, on the *English* side: But I never perceived any Impediment of Building, or having Ships in *Ireland*, but mens own indisposition thereunto, either for not having Stock for so chargeable a Work, or not having Workmen of sorts enough to fit out a Ship in all particulars; as for that they could hire Ships cheaper from the *Dutch*, than to build them; or, that the *Irish* had rather eat Potatos and Milk on dry Land, than contest with the Wind and Waves with better Food; or that there is not encouragement, to a full Employment, for an able Ship-wright to reside in *Ireland*. Neverthelesse at this day there belongs to several Ports of *Ireland* Vessels between 10 and 200 Tuns, about 8000 Tuns of several sorts and Sizes: And there are Five Light-Houses erected for the safety of sailing upon the Coasts.

Concerning the *Ambergreece*, taken upon the *Western* Coasts of *Ireland*, I could never verreceive any clear ſatisfaction, neither of its Odor, nor any other Vertue, nor what uſe was or could be made of that Stuff which has been ſo call'd, which is of ſeveral Appearances.

What is ſaid of the Herb *Mackenbory*, is fabulous, only that 'tis a Tythemal, which will purge furiouſly, and of which there are vaſt quantities in that part of *Kerry* call'd *Deſmond*, where the *Arbutus*-Tree groweth in great numbers and beauty.

There be in *Ireland* not ten Iron Furnaces, but above 20 Forges and Bloomeries, and but one Lead-work, which was ever wrought, tho many in view, which the pretended Patents of them have hindred the working of. There is alſo a place in *Kerry*, fit for one Allum-work, attempted, but not fully proceeded upon.

There are in the *Weſt* of *Ireland*, about 20 Gentlemen, who have engaged in the *Pilchard*-fiſhing, and have among them all about 160 Saynes, wherewith they ſometimes take about 4000 Hogſhheads of *Pilchards per Ann.* worth about 10,000 *l.* *Cork*, *Kingſale*, and *Bantry* are the beſt places for eating of Freſh-Fiſh, tho *Dublin* be not, or need not be ill ſupplied with the ſame.

The

The Clothing-Trade is not arrived to what it was before the late Rebellion. And the Art of making the excellent, thick, ſpungy, warm Coverlets, ſeems to be loſt, and not yet recovered.

Near *Colrane* is a *Salmon*-Fiſhing, where ſeveral Tuns of *Salmon* have been taken at one Draught, and in one Seaſon.

The *Engliſh* in *Ireland* before *Henry* the VII's time, lived in *Ireland* as the *Europians* do in *America*, or as ſeveral Nations do now upon the ſame Continent; ſo as an *Engliſhman* was not puniſhable for killing an *Iriſh-man*, and they were governed by different Laws; the *Iriſh* by the *Brehan*-Law, and the *Engliſh* there by the Laws of *England*.

Regiſters of Burials, Births and Marriages, are not yet kept in *Ireland*, though of late begun in *Dublin*, but imperfectly.

Engliſh in *Ireland*, growing poor and diſcontented, degenerate into *Iriſh*; *& vice verſa*; *Iriſh*, growing into Wealth and Favour, reconcile to the *Engliſh*.

Eleven *Iriſh* Miles make 14 *Engliſh*, according to the proportion of the *Iriſh* Perch of 21 Feet, to the *Engliſh* of 16½.

The

The admeasurement of Land in *Ireland*, hath hitherto been made with a Circumferencer, with a Needle of $3\frac{2}{3}$ long, as the most convenient Proportion; but 'twill be henceforth better done by the help of some old Geometrical Theoremes, joyn'd with this new property of a Circle, demonstrated by Dr. *R. Wood*.

The DIAGRAM.

ALtho the *Protestants* of *Ireland*, be to *Papists*, as three to eight; yet, because the former live in Cities and Towns, and the *Scots* live all in and about five of the 32 Counties of *Ireland*; It seems, in other open Counties, and without the Corporations, that the *Irish* and *Papists* are twenty to one.

A Report from the Council of Trade in *Ireland*, to the Lord Lieutenant and Council, which was drawn by Sir *William Petty*.

IN Obedience to your Lordship's Act of Council, of January *the 20th. 1675. we have spent several days in considering how, as well the Wealth of this Kingdom in general, as the Money thereof in particular may be increased. And in order thereunto, we have first set down to the best of our knowledge, the state of this Kingdom in reference to Trade.* Secondly, *We have noted such Inferences from the same, as do shew the several Causes of the smalness of Trade, want of Money, and the general Poverty of this Nation. And in the last place, we have offered such general Remedies and Expedients, in the respective Cases, as may be obtained and practised, without any new Law to be made in* Ireland. *And we are ready so to inlarge upon the Branches we have offered,*

offered, as to make ſuch of our Propoſals practicable, as your Lordſhips ſhall pleaſe to ſelect and approve of for that purpoſe.

March the 25th. 1676.

Conſiderations relating to the Improvement of IRELAND.

1. THE whole Territory of *Ireland* conſiſts of about 12 Millions of Acres (*Engliſh* Meaſure) of Arrable, Meadow, and good Paſture Land; with about two Millions of Rocky, Boggy, and Scrubby Paſture, commonly call'd Unprofitable, (tho not altogether ſuch): The reſt being abſolute Boggs, Loughs, Rocks, Sands, Strands, Rivers and High-ways, *&c.* Of all which, ſeveral Lands, the yearly Rent (comprehending Their Majeſties Quit-Rents, Tythes and Tenants Improvements) is ſuppoſed to be about 900,000 *l.* and worth to be purchaſed at Nine Millions.

2. The value of all the Houſing in *Ireland*, which have one or more Chimneys in them, (excluding all Cabbins which have none) is ſuppoſed to be Two Millions and a half.

3. The

3. The Cattel and Live-Stock, Three Millions.

4. Corn, Furniture, Merchandiſe, Shipping, *&c.* about One Million.

5. The Coyned and Currant Money, now running in Trade, is between 300, and 350,000 *l.* or the 50th part of the value of the whole Kingdom, which we ſuppoſe to be about 16 Millions.

6. The number of people in *Ireland* is about 1100,000, *viz.* Three Hundred Thouſand *Engliſh*, *Scotch*, and *Welch Proteſtants*, and 800,000 *Papiſts*, whereof ¼th are Children unfit for Labour, and about 75,000 of the Remainder are, by reaſon of their Quality and Eſtates, above the neceſſity of Corporal Labour; ſo as there remains 750,000 Labouring Men and Women, 500,000 whereof do perform the preſent Work of the Nation.

7. The ſaid 1100,000 people do live in about 200,000 Families or Houſes, whereof there are but about 16,000 which have more than one Chimney in each; and about 24,000 which have but one; all the other Houſes, being 160,000, are wretched naſty Cabbins, without Chimney, Window or Door ſhut, and worſe than thoſe of the Savage *Americans*, and wholly unfit for the making

making Merchantable Butter, Cheeſe, or the Manufactures of Woollen, Linnen or Leather.

8. The Houſes within the City and Liberties of *Dublin*, are under 5,000, *viz.* in the City 1150. And the Ale-Houſes within the ſame about 1200. And it ſeems, that in other Corporations and Countrey Towns, the proportion of Ale-Houſes is yet greater than in *Dublin*, *viz.* about $\frac{1}{3}$ of the whole.

9. The Counties, Baronies and Pariſhes, of *Ireland*, are now become marvellouſly unequal, ſo as ſome are twenty times as big as others, the County of *Cork* ſeeming in reſpect of people and Pariſhes to be $\frac{1}{8}$th of the whole Kingdom, and other Counties not being above the 20th part of the County of *Cork*; It hath been found very difficult to get fit perſons for Sheriffs, and Juries; and the often holding of Aſſizes and Quarter-Seſſions in the ſaid ſmaller Counties, hath been found an unneceſſary burthen upon them.

10. There are now in *Ireland* 32 Counties, 252 Baronies, and 2278 Pariſhes; ſo as the number of Sheriffs, and Sub-Sheriffs, Sheriff Bailiffs, High and Petty-Conſtables, are about three thouſand Perſons, whereof

not

not above $\frac{1}{10}$ are *Engliſh* or *Proteſtants.* So as the remainder (being about 2700) are *Iriſh Papiſts,* and are the Civil Militia of this Kingdom, and have the executing of all Decrees of Courts, and of Juſtices of the Peaces Warrants.

11. This Civil Militia, and the reſt of the *Iriſh Papiſts* being about 800,000, are influenced and guided by about 3000 Prieſts and Fryars, and they governed by their Biſhops and Superiors, who are for the moſt part, of the Old *Iriſh* Gentry, men of Foreign Education, and who depend upon Foreign Princes and Prelates, for Benefices and Preferments.

12. The *Iriſh Papiſts* (beſides Sundays and the 29 Holidays appointed by the Law) do one place with another, obſerve about 24 days more in the year, in which they do no Corporal Labour, ſo as they have but about 266 Working-days; whereas Proteſtants not ſtrictly obſerving all the Legal Holy-days, by a total forbearing of Labour, have in effect 300 Working-days in the year, that is, 34 days more than the Papiſts, or at leaſt five of ſix days in each, or $\frac{1}{11}$ part of the whole year.

13. The expence of the whole people of *Ireland* is about four Millions *per Ann.* the

the $\frac{1}{5}$ part whereof being 80,000 *l.* and the Quarter of Annual Houſe-Rent being about 60,000 *l.* together with 450,000 *l.* more, being the value of half a years Rent, Tythes and Quit-Rent, do make 590,000 l. as that ſum of Money which will compleatly and plentifully drive the Trade of this Kingdom.

14. The value of the Commodities exported out of *Ireland*, and the Fraight of the Shipping imployed in the Trade of this Nation, together with the fiſhing of *Herrings*, is about Five Hundred Thouſand pounds *per Annum.*

15. The value of the Eſtates in *Ireland* of ſuch perſons as do uſually live in *England*; the Intereſt of Debts of *Ireland*, due and payable to *England*; the pay of the Forces of *Ireland*, now in *England*; the Expence and Penſions of Agents and Sollicitors commonly reſiding in *England* about *Iriſh* Affairs; the Expence of *Engliſh* and *Iriſh* Youth now upon their Education beyond the Seas; and laſtly, the ſuppoſed Profit of the two great Farms now on Foot, do altogether make up near 200,000 *l. per Ann.* as a Debt payable to *England* out of *Ireland*.

16. The value of the Cattel, *viz.* live Oxen and Sheep, carried out of *Ireland* into

England

England, was never more than 140,000 l. *per Annum*; the Fraight, Hides, Tallow, and Wooll of the said live Cattel, were worth about 60,000 l. of the said 140,000 l. And the value of the Goods imported out of *England* into *Ireland* (when the Cattel-Trade was free) was between Treble and Quadruple, to the neat value of the Ox, and Sheeps Flesh transported from hence into *England*.

17. The Customs of Exported and Imported Goods, between *England* and *Ireland*, substracted from the Excise thereof, was in the freest Trade, about 32,000 *l.* *per Ann.*

Inferences from the Premisses.

1. BY comparing the Extent of the Territory with the number of people, it appears that *Ireland* is much underpeopled; for as much as there are above 10 Acres of good Land to every Head in *Ireland*; whereas in *England* and *France* there are but four, and in *Holland* scarce one.

2. That if there be 250,000 spare Hands capable of Labour, who can earn 4 or five l. *per*

per Ann. one with another, it follows that the people of *Ireland*, well employed, may earn one Million *per Ann.* more than they do now, which is more than the years Rent of the whole Country.

3. If an House with Stone-Walls, and a Chimney well covered, and half an Acre of Land well ditched about, may be made for 4 or 5 *l.* or thereabouts; then $\frac{2}{3}$ of the spare hands of *Ireland* can in one years time build and fit up 160,000 such Houses and Gardens, instead of the like number of the wretched Cabbins above-mentioned: And that in a time when a Foreign-Trade is most dead and obstructed, and when Money is most scarce in the Land.

4. The other third part of the said spare hands within the same year (besides the making of Bridges, Harbors, Rivers, High-ways, *&c.* more fit for Trade) are able to plant as many Fruit and Timber-Trees, and also Quick-set Hedges, as being grown up, would distinguish the Bounds of Lands, beautifie the Countrey, shade and shelter Cattel, furnish Wood, Fuel, Timber and fruit, in a better manner than ever was yet known in *Ireland* or *England.* And all this in a time when Trade is dead, and Money most scarce.

5. If

5. If the Gardens belonging to the Cabbins abovementioned, be planted with Hemp and Flax, according to the preſent Statute, there would grow 120,000 *l.* worth of the ſaid Commodities, the Manufactures whereof, as alſo of the Wooll and Hides now exported, would by the labour of the ſpare hands above-mentioned, amount to above One Million *per Annum* more than at preſent.

6. The multitude and proportion of Alehouſes above-mentioned, is a ſign of want of Employment in thoſe that buy, no leſs than thoſe that ſell the Drink.

7. There being but 800 Thouſand Papiſts in *Ireland*, and little above 2,000 Prieſts; It is manifeſt that 500 Prieſts may, in a competent manner, Officiate for the ſaid number of People and Pariſhes. And that two Popiſh Biſhops (if any at all be neceſſary) may as well Govern the ſaid 500 Prieſts, and two Thouſand Pariſhes; as the 26 Biſhops of *England* do Govern near Ten Thouſand Pariſhes.

8. If the Proteſtants, according to the preſent practice and underſtanding of the Law, do work one tenth part of the Year more than the Papiſts: And that there be be 750 Thouſand working People in *Ireland*,

land, whereof about 600 Thousand Papists. It follows that the Popish Religion takes off 60 Thousand workers, which, at about 4 *l. per Annum* each, is about 250 Thousand Pounds *per Annum* of it self; besides the Maintenance of 25 Hundred superfluous Churchmen, which at 20 *l. per Annum* each, comes to fifty thousand pounds *per Annum* more.

9. The Sheriffs of *Ireland* at 100 *l. per Annum*, the High Constables at 20 *l. per Annum*, and the Petty Constables at 10 *l. per Annum*, each, being all *English* Protestants (with some other incident Charges for the Administration of Justice) may be sallarated and defrayed for thirty thousand Pounds *per Annum*, consistent with His Majesty's present Revenue, Forces, *&c.* which said Sallaries, may also be lessened, by Uniting some of the smaller Counties, Baronies and Parishes, according to the proportion of People Inhabiting within them.

10. If there be not 350 Thousand Pounds Coyned Money in *Ireland*; And if 590 Thousand Pounds (or near double what there now is) be requisite to drive the Trade thereof; then it follows, that there is not enough in *Ireland* to drive the Trade of the Nation.

11. If

11. If the Lands of *Ireland* and Housing in Corporations, be worth above 10 Millions to be now sold (and if less than One Million of stock will drive all the Trade afore-mentioned, that *Ireland* is capable off) reckoning but two returns *per Annum*: It is certain that the lesser part of the said Ten Millions worth of real Estate, being well contrived into a Bank of Credit, will with the Cash yet remaining, abundantly answer all the ends of Domestick Improvements, and Foreign Traffick whatsoever.

12. If the whole substance of *Ireland* be worth 16 Millions, as above said: If the customs between *England* and *Ireland*, were never worth above thirty two thousand Pounds *per Annum*: If the Titles of Estates in *Ireland*, be more hazardous and expensive, for that *England* and *Ireland* be not under one Legislative Power: If *Ireland* till now, hath been a continual Charge to *England*; If the reducing the late Rebellion did cost *England* three times more in men and money, than the substance of the whole Countrey, when reduced, is worth: If it be just, that men of *English* Birth and Estates, living in *Ireland*, should be represented in the Legislative Power; and that the *Irish* should not be judged by those who, they

they pretend, do usurp their Estates: It then seems just and convenient, That both Kingdoms should be United and Governed by one Legislative Power. Nor is it hard to shew how this may be made practicable, nor to satisfy, repair, or silence those who are Interested or Affected to the contrary.

13. In the mean time, it is wonderful that men born in *England*, who have Lands granted to them by the King, for service done in *Ireland* to the Crown of *England*, when they have occasion to reside or negotiate in *England*, should by their Countrymen, Kindred and Friends there, be debarred to bring with them out of *Ireland* food whereupon to live, nor suffered to carry money out of *Ireland*, nor to bring such Commodities as they fetch from *America* directly home, but round about by *England*, with extream hazard and loss, and be forced to trade only with Strangers, and become unacquainted with their own Country; especially when *England* gaineth more than it loseth by a free Commerce; as exporting hither three times as much as it receiveth from hence: Insomuch as 95 *l.* in *England*, was worth about 100 *l.* of the like Money in *Ireland*, in the freest time of Trade.

14. It

14. It is conceived that about $\frac{1}{3}$*d* of the Imported Manufactures, might be made in *Ireland*, and $\frac{1}{3}$*d* of the remainder might be more conveniently had from Foreign parts, than out of *England*, and conſequently that it is ſcarce neceſſary at all for *Ireland* to receive any goods of *England*, and not convenient to receive above $\frac{1}{4}$*th* part from hence of the whole which it needeth to Import, the value whereof is under 100 Thouſand Pounds *per Annum.*

The application of the Premiſſes, in order to remedy the defects and impediments of the Trade of Ireland

1. Foraſmuch as the conſideration of Raiſing Money, hath already, and ſo lately, been before your Lordſhips; therefore without giving this Board any further trouble concerning the ſame: We humbly offer, in order to the regulation of the ſeveral ſpecies thereof; That whereas Weighty Plate pieces, together with Ducatoons, which eſtimate to be three quarters of the Money now currant in *Ireland*; do already paſs at proportionable Rates; and for that all other ſpecies of Silver Money, are neither rated proportionably to the ſaid weighty

pieces,

pieces, nor to one another; That Whole, Half and Quarter Cobbs of Sterling Silver (if light) may paſs at 5 *s.* 7 *d. per* Ounce; but that the other Species of courſer Silver, as the Perrues, *&c.* may paſs as Commodity, or at 5 *s. per* Ounce, until there ſhall be conveniency for new Coyning thereof into ſmaller Money.

2. That forthwith Application may be made unto *England*, to reſtore the Trade from the Plantations, and between the two Kingdoms (and particularly that of Cattel) as heretofore; and in the mean time to diſcover and hinder, by all means poſſible, the carrying of Bullion out of *Ireland* into *England*; to the end that thoſe in *England* who are to receive Moneys from hence, may be neceſſitated to be very earneſt in the ſaid Negotiation.

3. That Endeavours be uſed in *England*, for the Union of the Kingdoms under one Legiſlative Power, proportionably, as was heretofore and ſucceſſively done in the caſe of *Wales*.

4. For reducing Intereſt from Ten to Five, or Six, *per Centum*, for diſpoſing moneyed men to be rather Merchants than Uſurers, rather to trade than purchaſe, and to prevent the bad and uncertain pay-

ments,

ments, which Gentlemen are forced to make unto Tradesmen, whose Stock and Credit is thereby soon buried in debts, not to be received without long and expensive Suits, and that a Bank of Land be forthwith contrived and countenanced.

5. That the Act of State which mitigates and compounds, for the Costoms of some Foreign goods, purposely made high to hinder their Importation, and to encourage the Manufacture of them here, be taken into consideration (at least before it be renewed).

6. That the Lord Lieutenant and Council, as also the Nobility, Courts of Justice and Officers of the Army, and other Gentlemen in and about *Dublin*, may by their engagement and example, discountenance the use of some certain Foreign Commodities, to be pitched upon by your Lordships: And that Gentlemen and Freeholders in the Country, at their Assizes, and other Country meetings; and that the Inhabitants of all Corporations, who live in Houses of above two Chimneys in each, may afterwards do the same.

7. That there be a Corporation for the Navigation of this Kingdom, and that other Societies of men may be instituted,

who

who ſhall undertake and give ſecurity to carry on the ſeveral Trades and Manufactures of *Ireland*; and to ſee that all goods Exported to Foreign Markets, may be faithfully wrought and packt: Which Societies may direct themſelves, by the many ſeveral propoſals and reports formerly, and of late made by the Council of Trade, and which they are now again ready to enlarge and accommodate to the ſaid ſeveral propoſals reſpectively, and more particularly to the Manufactures of Woollen, Linnen, and Leather.

8. That the Corporations of *Ireland*, may be obliged to engage no Manufactures, but according to their Primitive Inſtructions; which was to carry on ſuch great works, as exceeded the ſtrength of ſingle Perſons; and particularly that they may cauſe ſome ſuch like proportions of Yarn, Linnen, and Woollen, as alſo of Worſted, to be Spun, as Mr. *Hawkins* hath Propounded.

9. That the Pattents, which hinder the working of Mines may be conſidered.

10. That

10. That the Juſtices of Peace, may be admoniſhed to protect the Induſtrious, and not ſuffer their Labours to be interrupted by vexatious and frivolous Indictments.

11. That the Inhabitants of the wretched Cabbins in *Ireland*, may be encouraged to reform them; and alſo compelled thereunto, as an eaſy and Indulgent Committing for the Penalty of Nine-Pence *per* Sunday payable, by the Statute; and likewiſe to make Gardens, as the Statute for Hemp and Flax requires. And that other the wholeſome Laws againſt Idlers, Vagabonds, *&c.* may be applied to the prevention of Beggary and Thievery: Whereunto the orderly diſpoſing of the ſaid Cabbins into Townſhips would alſo conduce.

12. That the People be diſſuaded from the obſervations of ſuperfluous Holy-Days.

13. That the exorbitant Number of Popiſh-Prieſts and Fryars, may be reduced to a bare competency, as alſo the Number of Ale-houſes.

14. That

14. That the Conſtable, Sheriff, and Bailiffs, may alſo be *Engliſh* Proteſtants, (though upon Salary)

From all which, and from the ſettlement of Eſtates; it is to be hoped, that men ſeeing more advantage to live in Ireland *than elſewhere, may be invited to remove themſelves hither; and ſo ſupply the want of People, the greateſt and moſt fundamental defect of this Kingdom.*

CAROLUS

CAROLUS *Secundus, Dei Gratia,* Angliæ, Scotiæ, Franciæ *&* Hiberniæ *Rex, Fidei Defensor,* &c. *Omnibus ad quos præsentes literæ pervenerint salutem. Cum prædilectus, perquam fidelis consanguineus & Consiliarius noster* Jacobus *Dux* Ormondiæ *in regno nostro Hiberniæ, qui plurima egregia servitia serenissimo patri nostro Beatissimæ memoriæ in eodem regno, in loco & qualitate Domini Locum-tenentis generalis & generalis Gubernatoris ejusdem regni nostri per multos annos in temporibus maximæ calamitatis summa cum prudentia & integritate præstiterit, ac sese fidum & fortem assertorem Coronæ Angliæ jurium continuè comprobaverit, utpote qui dicto patri nostro per totam flagitiosam illam Subditorum suorum nuperam defectionem, magnanimiter adhærescens in prælio primus & audax, in consilio prudens, & nemini secundus extiterit; atque nobis etiam tum extremis exilii nostri angustiis, tum restitutione nostra, inseparabilis & indefatigabilis adfuerit comes & adjutor: Nos præmissa perpendendentes æquum duximus, in tesseram favoris nostri, eundem Ducem Ormondiæ Locum-tenentem nostrum generalem regni nostri Hiberniæ prædicti, & generalem in eodem regno Gubernatorem constituere.* Sciatis, *quod nos de provi-*

provida circumspectione & industria præfati Jacobi Ducis Ormondiæ plurimum confitentes de advisamento Concilii *nostri & ex certa Scientia & mero motu nostris assignavimus, fecimus, ordinavimus, constituimus & deputavimus & per præsentes assignamus, facimus, ordinamus, constituimus & deputamus eundem Ducem Ormondiæ Locum-tenentem nostrum generalem regni nostri Hiberniæ prædict' necnon Gubernator' nostrum generalem regni nostri illius,* Habendum *tenendum, gaudendum, exercend' & occupand' offic' præd' præfato Jacobo Duci Ormondiæ una cum omnibus & singulis vad' feod' stipend' & assocation' eidem officio spectan' & pertinen' durante beneplacito nostro; Dantes & concedentes eidem Locum-tenenti nostro generali &* Gubernatori *nostro generali plenam tenore præsentium potestatem & authoritatem ad pacem nostram & ad leges & consuetudines regni nostri prædict' custodiend' & custodire faciend' & ad omnes & singulos Ligeos nostros tam Anglicos quàm Hibernicos dicti regni nostri ac alios quoscunque, per nos super dictum Locum-tenent' nostrum generalem & Gubernatorem nostrum generalem, stipendiatos & alias quascunque personas, ibidem contra nos, aut pacem, consuetudinem & leges prædict' qualecunque delinquend' & contraveniend' juxta eorum demerita, secundum leges & consuetudines*

nes

nes prædictas, viis & modis quibus melius pro honore & proficuo nostro fieri poterit: ac pro bana gubernatione dicti regni nostri ac Ligeorum & Subditor' nostrorum ibidem juxta discretionem dicti Locum-tenentis nostri general' & Gubernatoris nostri general castigand' & puniend' ac puniri & castigari faciend' necnon ordinationes & Statuta pro salvo & bono regimine regni nostri prædict' juxta advisamentum consilii nostri ibidem ordinand' Statuend' & stabiliend' ac super inde proclamationes faciend' debitæque executioni demandand' ac quoscunque contravenientes & delinquentes castigand' & incarcerand' atque incarceratos solvend' & deliberand' Necnon ad recipiend' & admittend' per dictum advisament' Consilii nostri ad fidem & pacem nostram, tam Anglicos quàm Hibernicos, & alios quoscunque infra prædict' regnum nostrum Hiberniæ habitantes vel commorantes intutand' seu commorand' qui nobis, legibus nostris consuetud' prædict' Rebelles & contrarii extiterint aut existunt vel existent; & ad concedend' faciend' & dand' per hujusmodi advisament' plenam pardonationem, remissionem, relaxationem & absolutionem tam general' quàm Specialem, illis & eorum cuilibet hujusmodi pardonationem petent' aut habere volen' ac sectam pacis nostræ quæ ad nos pertinet tam pro Homicid Rober' Felon' Murdr' Rapt' mulierum,

rum, Latrociniis, falsis allegation' adhæsion' inimicis Utlagar' transgression' contempt' & aliis offensis quibuscunque in dicto regno nostro per aliquas hujusmodi personas ante hæc tempora fact' seu in posterum faciend' & eorum forisfactur' & firmam pacem nostram eis & eorum cuilibet literas patentes sub magno sigillo quo utimur in regno nostro prædicto in forma debita concedend' donand' & deliberand' ac etiam eosdem alios quoscunque ad fines & redemptiones hujusmodi offens' & eorum quamlibet qui fines & redemptiones facere debuerunt seu voluerunt accipiend' & recipiend' Et singul' personis juxta leges & consuetudines præd' justitiam faciend' & fieri mandand' Ac etiam ad universos & singulos tam Anglos Rebelles quàm Hibernicos dicti regni nostri & alios quoscunque dictum regnum nostrum in posterum invadend' ac ipsum regnum nostrum subditosque nostros ejusdem deprædare, gravare seu alio modo destruere seu devastare intendent' ac se juxta leges, & consuetudines prædict' justificare volentes, si necesse fuerit, cum potestate nostra Regia, ac aliis viis & modis, quibus melius fieri poterit juxta eorum demerita puniend' & si opus fuerit ultimo supplicio demandand' ac Subditos nostros providè commovend' convocand' & levand' ac cum eisdem Subditis nostris sic levat' contra dictos Rebelles congrediend'

eosque

eosque invadend' vincend' & castigand' & si opus fuerit terr' ipsorum aliis qui nobis servire volunt & intendunt de advisamento prædict' locand' & demittend' Ac etiam cum eis pacificand' & pacem componend' ac ipsos paci nostræ restorand' toties quoties in præmissis vel circa ea opus fuerit. Proviso *tamen semper, quod super quamlibet talem dimissionem & location' per præfat' Jacobum Ducem Ormondiæ ac prædict' advisament' Consilii nostri præd' in posterum virtute harum literarum nostrarum patentiu' faciend' annual' reddit' superinde debit' sit nobis, hæredibus & Successoribus nostris, omnino reservat'* Damus insuper *& concedimus eidem Jacobo Duci Ormondiæ Locum-tenenti nostro generali & Gubernatori nostro generali, tenore præsentium, plenam potestatem & authoritatem omnes proditiones, necnon felon' murdr' rapt' mulier' ibidem & alias causas & offensam quascunque per Subditos ejusdem regni nostri Hiberniæ, vel alios ibidem residend' commiss' sive comittend' prodition' quæ destructionem vitæ nostræ concernerunt tantummodo except' pardonand' abolend' remittend & relaxand' literasque nostras Patentes sub dicto magno Sigillo nostro superinde cuicunque personæ regni nostri Hiberniæ præd' nomine nostro concedend' componend' & ad easdem Sigilland' Cancellar' nostro vel Custod'*

stod' Sigilli dicti nostri regni nostri Hiberniæ mandand' tradend' & deliberand'. Damus *præterea & concessimus eidem Jacobo Duci Ormondiæ Locum-tenenti nostro generali & Gubernatori nostro generali, plenam potestatem & authoritatem quoscunque de Stirpe Anglicano existend' in officio in regno prædict' tam secundo Baroni Scaccar' nostri & quorumcunque computand' ac aliar' officiar' perficere, ipsosque officiar' intra regnum nostrum prædictum facere, deputare & constituere ;* Habendum *eis & eorum cuilibet & quibuslibet, durante beneplacito nostro, & quamdiu in eodem se bene gerunt ad libitum ejusdem Locum-tenentis nostri general' & Gubernatoris nostri general' una cum vad' & regard' eisdem officiar' ab antiquo debit' & consuet' offic' Cancellar' Thesaurar' Subthesaurar' Justiciar' utriusque Banci & Capital' Baron' Scaccar' nostri offic' Magistri Rotulorum ac offic' Thesaurar' ad gueram offic' Marescall' offic' magistri ordination' Clerici de le Checque' offic' præsiden' Munster & Connaght ac officium Attor' & Sollicitator' nostri ejusdem regni nostræ Hiberniæ tantumodo except' Statut & Parliamen' Domini Henrici nuper Regis Angliæ Septimi Progenitor' nostri inclytæ memoriæ, Anno regni sui decimo, coram Edwardo Poyning Milite tunc deputato regni nostri Hiberniæ tent' edit' & provis' non obstante.* Concessimus

etiam

etiam præfato Locum-tenenti nostro generali potestatem quod ipse durante beneplacito nostro omnia officia Ecclesiastica, tam jurat' quam non jurat' viz. Vicar' Parsonat Præbendar' Cantur' Capell' Hospital' Dignitat' Archionat' & alia beneficia quæcunque nominatione Archiepiscopor' & Episcopor' tantum except' tam in Ecclesiis Cathedral' quam Collegiat' Hospitat' & Paroch' in quocunque loco in regnum nostrum Hiberniæ quocunque titulo jam vacan' seu in posterum ex causa quacunque vacare contingen' & ad præsentationem, collationem sive donationem nostram quocunque modo spectan' personis idoneis quibuscunque sibi placuerit dand' concedend' & conferend' & ad eadem omnia & Singula quorum ad nos præsentationis, donationis sive collationis spect' & pertinent, & stat' & possess' omnium & singulorum qui de eorum aliquibus possessionat' existunt ratificand' approband' & confirmand' ac privileg' libertat' imunitat' & concess' per prædecessores nostros quoscunque aut aliquos alios ante hæc tempora fact' sive concess' prout eidem Locum-tenenti nostro general' & gubernatori nostro general' per advisament' & consensu Consilii nostri in regno nostro præd' melius expedire videbitur ratificand' approband' & confirmand' Concessimus *insuper eidem Jacobo Duci Ormondiæ Locum-tenenti*

nenti nostro generali & gubernatori nostro General' potestat' & fidelit' provision' & renuntiation' Archiepiscopor' & Episcopor' in eodem regno nostro Hiberniæ, tempore præterito sive futuro, fact' ordinat' & consueta acceptand' faciend' ordinand' & constituend' ac omnia alia ad nos debit' nomine nostro recipiend' eisdem Archiepiscopis, Episcopis & ear' quilibet temporalia sua Cancellar' nostro regni nostri prædict' deliber' mandand' cum omnibus & singulis juribus Emolumen' proficuis & reven tionibus ratione vacationis deor' beneficior' dignitat' Archiepiscopat' sive Episcopat' nobis reservat' ac etiam Homag' omnium & singulorum tam Spiritual' quàm temporal' tenen' & Subditor' nostrorum quorumcunque in regno nostro prædicto nomine nostro recipiend' & terras & tenement' sua de hereditate sua Cancellar' nostro delibari mandand' manusque nostras exinde amovend' ac Victual' sufficien' & necessar' pro expens' Hospitii sui & soldar' suor' in quocunque infra dictum regnum Hiberniæ per provisor' Hospitii sui & alios Ministr' suos una cum carriag' sufficien' pro eisdem, tam infra libertates quàm extra, pro denar' suis rationabil' solvend' providend' & capiend juxta formam Statuti de hujusmodi provision' ante hæc tempora fact' nisi aliter per composition' fact' cum intutan' Com' infra partes vulgariter vocatos

The

The English Pale *aliosque Com' extra deces partes provisum sit aut post hac provideatur, quod præd Locum-tenens general' & Gubernator noster general' habeat vel habere possit summam pecuniæ annuatim in dicta compositione ante hæc limitat' pro compensatione & recompensatione pro hujusmodi Virtual' providend' & capiend' pro provisor' hospitii sui, quam quidem compositionem censemus observand' pro beneficio Subditor' nostror' necnon ad Summonend' & Sumonire faciend' atque tenend' secundum Leges, Statut' & Consuetudin' regni nostri Hiberniæ prædict' unum duntaxat Parliament' quandoquidem sibi melius expediri videbitur, consensu tamen nostro in ea parte semper habit' & ad idem Parliament' prorogand' & adjournand' toties quoties necesse fuerit, & infra deos annos à tempore interceptionis ejusdem plenè determinand' & finiend' & quoscunque sic Summonit' absentes & non legitime impedit' mulctand' & puniend'* Concessimus *insuper dicto Locum-tenenti nostro general' & Gubernator' nostro' general' plenam & sufficien' authoritatem & potestat' ad omnimod' officiar' computabil' Thesaurar' & Subthesaurar' regni nostri prædict' duntaxat except' coram eisdem Thesaurar', Subthesaurar' nostris & Baron' Scaccarii nostri dicti regni nostri Hiberniæ, computare faciend' & ad hujusmodi comput' reddend'*

reddend' compelland' ac etiam ad inquirend' & inquiri faciend' viis & modis quibus melius sibi videbitur, faciend' de quibuscunque bonis & cattallis quæ fuer' ill' sive alior qui erga nos seu Progenitores *nostros forisfecerunt vel forisfacient, & à nobis concelat' existunt vel imposterum existent, & ad omnia & singula alia quæ ad offic' locum tenentis nostri generalis &* Gubernatoris *nostri generalis jure, usu & consuetud' regni nostri præd' pertinent aut pertinere deberent & pro bono regimine & Salvatione & pro bono custod' pacis regni nostri præd' & quiete populi nostri ibidem, & recuperatione jurium nostrorum in regno nostro Hiberniæ necessar' fuerit; Salvis super reservatis faciend' exercend' exequend' & ordinand' omnia alia nomine nostro & pro nobis in dicto regno nostro Hiberniæ faciend' exercend' & ordinand' sicut nos faceremus aut facere possemus si ibidem in propria persona nostra essemus.* Damus *insuper præfato Jacobo Duci Ormondiæ Locum tenenti nostro Generali & Gubernatori nostro generali potestatem & authoritatem Navibus nostris quibuscunque aut aliis quæ circa littora dicti regni nostri Hiberniæ sunt in Servitio nostro, aut in posterum quacunque occasione erunt & mittentur pro defensione dicti regni nostri Hiberniæ, imperand' & utend' pro servitio nostro & tutamine dicti regni nostri,*

nostri, prout ipse secundum discretionem suam & per advisamentum Concilii nostri ejusdem regni nostri Hiberniæ visum, erit nisi nos Special' Commission' nostra aut Admiralli nostri Angliæ ordinatione special' Gubernator' & Capitan' præd' Navium nostrarum aut aliis mittend' speciali instructione mandat' & servic' imperaverimus aut imperaverit. Constituimus etiam præfat. Jacobum Ducem Ormondiæ Gubernator' & Præfect. nostrum general' exercitûs nostri in dicto regno nostro Hiberniæ, tam præsentis quàm futuri, quàm diu nobis placuerit, cum Alacationibus inde debit' & consuet. Ac eidem Duci Præfecto generali exercitus nostri ibidem plenam potestatem & authoritatem concedimus faciend' constituend' & ordinand' leges, ordinationes & proclamationes de tempore in tempus, ut casus exegerit, pro bono regimine exercitus nostri prædict' ac omnes quorumcunque sub mandato & Gubernatione ejusdem præfectus generalis exercitûs nostri easdemque leges, ordinationes & proclamationes exequendi ac debitæ executioni mandand' ac etiam infligere, adjudicare & assidere timor' pœnas corporales, imprisonamenta, fines, forisfactur' ac omnes alias pœnas & penalitates quascunque in & super omnes delinquentes sive offendentes contra hujusmodi leges, ordinationes & proclamationes qualis & quæ eidem Gubernatori

bernatori & præfecto nostro exercitûs nostri requisit' & necessar' fore videbuntur' Quæ omnia leges, ordinationes & proclamationes, sic ut præfert' faciend' observari volumus sub pœnis in eisdem continend'. Et ei damus potestatem & authoritatem utendi & exercendi infra regnum nostrum prædictum si opus fuerit, lege Marifcal' Sive Martial' necnon substituend' assignand' & appuntuand' sub se infra dictum regnum nostrum per literas nostras Patentes sub magno Sigillo nostro dict' regni nostri prædict' faciend' tot & tales Marriscallos, Commissarios & al' officiar' ad legem Armor' seu legem Martial' exercend' & exequend' prout præfat' Locum-tenenti nostro general' & Gubernator' nostro general' de tempore in tempus expedire videbit ad exercend' utend' & exequend' præd' leges, quoties opus & necesse fuerit, & juramenta præstare, aliaque omnia per se vel per alios facere, erigere, quæ ad leges prædictas exercend' aliqualiter pertineant. Et quia valde necessar' nobis videatur ut præfat' Locum-tenens noster generalis & Gubernator noster generalis pro negotiis nostris magni momenti personam nostram Regiam in propria persona sua sicut nobis visum fuerit attendat' Ideo ulterius *damus, & per præsentes præfato Jacobo Duci Ormondiæ Locum-tenenti & Gubernator' nostro general' plenam potestatem & autho-*

authoritatem concedimus nominand' & assignand' per literas nostras Patentes sub magno Sigillo nostro, dicti regni nostri Hiberniæ nomine nostro, tam nunc quàm de tempore in tempus imposterum, conficiend' quamcunque aut quoscunque dictus Locum-tenens & Gubernator noster general' in hac parte idoneum sive idoneos duxerit fore deputat' vel deputatos quocunque nomine assignatos durante beneplacito nostro pro Gubernatione dicti regni nostri Hiberniæ in absentia sua, donec idem Locum-tenens & Gubernator noster in dictum regn' Hiberniæ gubernatione ejusdem ut præfert' redierit, volentes tamen quod in eisdem literis Patentibus alicui personæ seu personis sicut præfert' faciend' Deputat' aut Deputatos in absentia sua tantum provis' & nomine nostro mand' sit quod non licebit alicui tal' Deputat' vel deputatis Thesaurar' seu pecunias nostras cuicunque solvere vel erogare, authoritat' seu warrant' ipsius Deputat' vel ipsorum Deputat' tantum sed quod omnia erod' mandat' & Warrant' per Thesaur' & pecuniis nostris per ipsum fient & Signabunt non solum manu propria præfat' Deput' vel præfator' Deputator' sed etiam manibus prædilectorum & fidel' Consiliar' nostrorum Magistri Curiæ Wardor' Capital' Baron' Scaccar' nostri' Cancellar' Scaccar' nostri & primar' Secretarii nostri ibidem pro tempore existente vel saltem

ſaltem manibus duorum illorum. Damus *ulterius universis, ſingulis Archiepiſcopis, Ducibus, Comitibus, Vice-Comitibus, Epiſcopis, Baron' Juſticiar' Militibus, liberis hominibus & aliis Subditis noſtris de regno noſtro prædict' firmè in mandatis, quòd præfato Jacobo Duci Ormondiæ Locum-tenenti noſtro general & Gubernatori noſtro general' in eodem regno noſtro intendentes ſive aſſidentes, auxiliantes & conſultantes, ac ipſius mandatis in omnibus prout decet aut decebit obedientes ſint, aliquo ſtatut' Actu, Ordinatione, proviſione, jure, uſu, conſuetudine ſive reſtriction' in contrar' inde fact' edit' ordinat' ſive provis' aut aliqua alia re, cauſa vel materia quacunque in aliquo non obſtante.* In cujus *rei teſtimonium has literas noſtras fieri fecimus Patentes Teſte meipſo apud Weſtmonaſter' Viceſſimo primo die Februarii Ann. regni noſtri quarto decimo*

Per ipſum Regem

BARKER.

Inrotulat' in Rotulis patentibus Cancellariæ Hiberniæ de Ann. regni Regis Caroli Secundi decimo quarto & Examinat' per

J. TEMPLE.

At

At the Court at *Hampton-Court*, *JUNE* 22. 1662.

Propositions to be consider'd of by his Majesty, concerning the governing of *Ireland*.

CHARLES *R.*

1. *THAT his Majesty may declare his express Pleasure, that no* Irish *Suit by way of reward be moved for by any of his Servants, or others, before the Ordinary Revenue there become, able to sustain the necessary charge of that Crown, and the Debts there of befully cleared.*

This is most reasonable, it standing with no sound rule of Judgment, to exercise the Acts of bounty in a place which doth not discharge it self, and will prove the readiest and most expedient way to recover his Majesties affairs thereby, thus carrying the Revenues in their natural Channell; and indeed this

this courſe being conſtantly purſu'd, will much encreaſe the annual profits above what they now are, and intirely draw the dependance of the inferiors from the great Lords upon his Majeſty, and ſo the intereſt and aſſurance the Crown ſhall have in the Natives thereof, be of no leſs conſequence and advantage than the very profits.

2. *That there be an expreſs Caveat entred with the Secretary, Signet, Privy Seal and Great Seal here, That no Grant, of what nature ſoever, concerning* Ireland, *be ſuffered to paſs, till the Lord Lieutenant be made acquainted, and it firſt paſs the ſeal of that Kingdom, according to the uſual manner.*

This will be of great intelligence and ſafety to his Majeſty; for on the one ſide he will clearly ſee into the true inward value all things, which formerly, albeit of very great worth, have from ſo great a diſtance ſlipt away here, as little underſtood by the Crown; as is acknowledged by thoſe that obtain them; who generally, in theſe cauſes, ſacrifice rather to their own Wit, than the Goodneſs and Bounty of Kings. And on the other ſide, nothing can paſs to the diſadvantage of the Crown; and proper

Mini-

Minifters, inftructed with thefe Affairs, may be immediately faulted and juftly called to a fevere Account for their Negligence and Unfaithfulnefs therein; which will give them good reafon to look more narrowly into his Majefties Rights, and their own Duties.

3. *That His Majefty Signify his Royal Pleafure, that fpecial Care be taken hereafter, that fufficient and credible Perfons be chofen to fupply fuch Bifhopricks as fhall be void, or admitted of his Privy Councel, or fit as Judges, and ferve of his learned Councel there; that he will vouchfafe to hear the advice of his Lieutenant before he refolve of any in thefe cafes, that the Lieutenant be commanded to inform his Majefty truly and impartially, of every mans particular Diligence, and Care in his Service there, to the end his Majefty may truly and gracioufly reward the well-deferving, by calling them home to better preferment here.*

This will advantage the fervice; it being altogether impoffible for the Lieutenant, be he never fo induftrious and able, to adminifter the publick Juftice of fo great a Kingdom, without the round affiftance of other able and well-affected Minifters. This will encourage the beft men to fpend their

their ſtronger years there, when they ſhall ſee their elder age recompenſed with eaſe and profit in their own native Soyl ; and content and ſettle the Natives, when they find themſelves cared for, and put in the hands of diſcreet and good men to govern them.

4. *That no particular Complaints of Injuſtice or Oppreſſion be admitted here against any, unleſs it appears, That the Party made firſt his Addreſs unto the Lieutenant.*

This is but juſtice to the Lieutenant, who muſt needs in ſome meaſure be a delinquent, if the complaint be true;for that he ought as in chief, univerſally to take care that his Majeſties Juſtice be truly and fully adminiſtred; and therefore good reaſon that his Judgment ſhould be informed, and his integrity firſt tryed, before either be impeached ; Nay, it is but juſtice to the Government it ſelf, which would be exceedingly Scandalized through the liberty of complaints, and the Miniſters therein extreamly diſcouraged upon any petty matter, to be drawn to anſwer here, when as the thing it ſelf is for the moſt part either Injurious or ſuch as the party might have received good ſatisfaction for at his own doors : but where the complaint appea-

appeareth formally grounded, that is, where due application hath been made to the Lieutenant, without any help or relief to the party, as may be pretended; let it in the name of God be throughly examined, and severely punished, wheresoever the fault prove to be; especially if it be found to be corrupt or malitious: for thus shall not his Majesty only magnify his own Justice, but either punish an unfaithful Minister, or a clamorous Complainer; and so his Service be better'd by either example.

5. *That no Confirmation of any Reversion of Office within that Kingdom be had, or any new Grant of Reversion hereafter to pass.*

That disposing of Places thus aforehand, much abates mens endeavours, who are many times stirred up to deserve eminently in the Commonwealth, in hope of those preferments; and being thus granted away, there is nothing left in their Eye, for them to expect and aim at, which might nourish and quicken those good desires in them, besides Places there closely and covertly passed, the persons are not for the most part so able and fitted to the Duties thereof, as when there is choice made out of many publick pretenders, which commonly occur,

cur, when they actually fall void by Death.

6. *That the Places in the Lieutenants Gift, as well in the Martial as Civil List, be left freely to his disposing; and that his Majesty may be graciously pleased not to pass them to any person, upon Suits made unto him here.*

This course held, preserves the Rights of the Lieutenants Place, and his Person in that Honour and Esteem which can only enable him to do service; and if the contrary happen, it is not only in diminution to him, but draws off all necessary dependance upon him, and regard that ought to be had of him, in all ready obedience in such things he shall command, for the Kings Service, when they shall discern that the natural Powers of the Place are taken from him, whereby he might kindle their chearful endeavours by the preferring and furnishing such as deserve those places.

7. *That no New Offices be erected within that Kingdom before such time as the Lieutenant be therewith acquainted; his opinion first required and certified accordingly.*

Suits

Suits of this Nature, however they pretend the publick, their chief end is the private Profit of the Propounder; and for the most part, in the Execution prove burthens, not benefits to the Subjects; therefore throughly to be understood before they pass, as more easy and less scandalous to the State, to be staid at first than afterwards recalled, and if they be really good, his Majesty may be better informed by his Lieutenants approbation, and so proceed with more assurance to the effecting thereof.

8. *That his Majesty would be pleased, not to grant any Licence of absence out of that Kingdom, to any Councillors, Bishops, Governours of any Province or County, or Officers of State, or of the Army, or to any of the Judges, or learned Council, but that it be left to his Lieutenant to give such Licence.*

This is but reasonable, because the Lord Lieutenant who is chiefly intrusted under his Majesty with the Care and Government of that Kingdom, is the most competent and proper Judge, who in publick employment may be spared, and how long, without Prejudice to his Majesty, or the publick.

9. *That all Propositions moving from the Lieutenant, touching matters of Revenue, may be*

be directed to the Lord Treasurer of England *only, and that the Addre∫s of all other Di∫patches for that Kingdom be by ∫pecial direction of his Maje∫ty applyed to one of the Secretaries ∫ingly, and his Maje∫ty, under his hand-Writing doth Specify, that his Maje∫ty will have this done by Mr. Secretary Nicholas.*

The∫e Propo∫itions made unto his Maje∫ty, by his Grace the Duke of *Ormond* Lord Steward of his Maje∫ty's Hou∫hold, and Lord Lieutenant of *Ireland*, were received and approved at the Council board, the 22 day of *June* 1662, there being pre∫ent the King's mo∫t excellent Maje∫ty his Royal Highne∫s the Duke of *York*, his Highne∫s Prince *Rupert*, the Lord Chancellor, the Lord Trea∫urer, Duke of *Albemarle*, Duke of *Ormond*, Marque∫s of *Dorche∫ter*, Lord Great Chamberlain, Lord Chamberlain, Earl of *Bark∫hire*, Earl of *Portland*, Earl of *Norwich*, Earl of *Angle∫ey*, Earl of *Lauderdail*, the Lord *Hatton*, Lord *Hollis*, Lord *A∫hly*, Sir William *Compton*, Mr. Trea∫urer, Mr. Vice Chamberlain, Mr Secretary Nicholas, Mr. Secretary *Morris*.

By His Maje∫ties Command,

EDWARD NICHOLAS.

At

At the Court at *Hampton-Court*,

JUNE 22. 1662.

Present,

The King's Most Excellent Majesty.
His Highness, the Duke of York.
His Highness, Prince Rupert.
Lord Chancellor.
Lord Treasurer.
Duke of Albemarl.
Duke of Ormond.
Marquess of Dorchester.
Lord Great-Chamberlain.
Earl of Berkshire.
Earl of Portland.
Earl of Norwich.
Earl of Anglesey.
Earl of Lauderdale.
Lord Hatton.
Lord Hollis.
Lord Ashly.
Sir William Compton.
Mr. Treasurer.
Mr. Vice-Chamberlain.
Mr. Secretary Nicholas.
Mr. Secretary Morris.

CHARLES *R.*

HIS Majesty's express pleasure is, That the Masters of Requests, and every of them, in their several Months of attendance

dance at Court, do Constantly observe these ensuing Directions, *viz.*

Not to move his Majesty in Petitions for any *Irish* Suit, by way of Reward, either for any of His Majesty's Servants, or others before the ordinary Revenue of that Kingdom become able to maintain the necessary Charge of that Crown, and the Debts thereof be fully cleared.

For any particular Complaint of Injustice or Oppression, pretended to be done there, unless it appear the Party made his first Address unto the Lord Lieutenant, for confirmation of any Reversion of Offices within that Kingdom, or any new Grant of Reversion hereafter; any places in the Lord-Lieutenants gift, either of the Civil or Military List, when any such shall fall void.

Any erection of a new Office in that Kingdom, before such time as the Lord-Lieutenant be therewithall acquainted, his Opinion required and certified back accordingly.

By His Majesty's Command,

EDWARD NICHOLAS.

CHARLES

CHARLES R.

THere being nothing more conducible to the quiet and ſafety of a Kingdom, than a frugal and regular ordering and diſpoſing of the Revenue that is to maintain the Publick Charge and Expence of the Government, both Civil and Military; We have thought fit, with the advice of our Council, upon a Proſpect made of all our Revenue, certain and caſual, and the juſt means in view upon the ſettlement of Eſtate in that Kingdom, now in hand for improveing thereof, to begin by this Eſtabliſhment, both to bring our Payments as near as may be to the compaſs of our Receipts, and to provide eſpecially for our Publick Affairs, by ſupporting Civil Juſtice and Government, and by maintaining our Forces in the preſent Strength and Fulneſs; intending hereafter, as our Charge may grow leſs, and our Means encreaſe, to extend our Favour and Bounty according to our gracious Inclinations, and the Merit of perſons, to the further encouragement of Particulars, as cauſe ſhall require: Whereof we have already given a proof, in the liberal Addition we have made to the Judges, for their better Support, in the impartial adminiſtration of Juſtice.

The

The LIST FOR CIVIL AFFAIRS;

Containing the ſeveral Entertainments, by the Year, of all Officers and others, ſerving in our Courts of Juſtice, in the ſeveral Provinces of *Ireland*: Officers belonging to the State; Officers of our Cuſtoms; Officers of the Exciſe: Creation-Money; with other Perpetuities and particular Payments for our Service; Which We require henceforth to be duely paid out of our Revenues there, by the Hands of our Vice-Treaſurer, or Receiver General for the time being, according to the Cautions here mentioned; the ſame to begin for, and from the Firſt day of *April*. 1666.

THESE following Payments are the conſtant Fees to be continued to the ſeveral Officers, without change from time to time.

	l.	s.	d.
The Right Honourable *Arthur*, Earl of *Angleſey*, Vice-Treaſurer, and General Receiver.	050	00	00

Sir

	l.	s.	d.
Sir *Robert Meredith* Kt. Chancellor of the Exchequer.	100	00	00
John Busse Esq; Lord Chief-Baron of the Exchequer.	600	00	00
Sir *Richard Kennedy* Kt. Second Baron of the Exchequer.	300	00	00
John Povey Esq; Third Baron of the Exchequer.	220	00	00
Sir *Audly Mervin* Kt. His Majesty's prime Serjeant at Law.	020	10	00
Sir *William Domvile* Kt. His Majesty's Attorney General.	075	06	00
Sir *John Temple* Kt. His Majesty's Sollicitor-General.	075	00	00
Philip Fernely, Esq; His Majesty's Chief-Remembrancer	030	00	00
Sir *James Ware*, Kt. His Majesty's Auditor-General, for his ancient Fee *per Ann.* 184 *l.* 6 s. 3 d. and for an Augmentation thereof, allowed by the former Establishment 50*l.* in all	234	06	03

Sir

	l.	s.	d.	
Sir *Allen Brodrick*, Kt. His Majesty's Surveyor-General.	060	00	00	*The Court of Exchequer.*
Frances Lee, Escheatour of the Province of *Leinster*.	006	13	04	
Escheatour of the Province of *Ulster*.	020	05	00	
Escheatour of the Province of *Munster*.	020	05	00	
Escheatour of the Province of *Connaght*.	020	05	00	
Henry Warren, Esq; Second Remembrancer.	007	17	06	
Nicholas Loftus, Esq; Clerk of the Pipe.	015	00	00	
Roger Moor, Esq; Chief-Chamberlain.	010	00	00	
Sir *Robert Kennedy*, Bar^t. Second Chamberlain.	005	00	00	
Maurice Keating, Controllor of the Pipe.	007	00	00	
John Longfield, Usher of the Exchequer, for his Fee *per Annum*, 2 *l.* 10 *s.* and for his allowance for Ink, for the Exchequer, 10 *l. per Annum.* In all, *per Annum.*	012	10	00	

Thomas

		l.	s.	d.
	Thomas Lea, Tranſcriptour and Forreign Oppoſer.	015	00	00
	Edward Ludlow, Summonitor of the Exchequer.	007	05	00
	John Burniſton, Marſhal of the four Courts.	004	00	00
	Sir *Theophilus Jones*, Kt. Clerk of the Pells.	030	00	00
	John Exham, Clerk of the firſt fruits, and twentieth parts.	027	10	00
	Thomas Gibſon, Cryer of the Court of Exchequer.	001	14	04
The Court of Kings Bench.	The Right Honourable *James*, Baron of *Santry*, Lord Chief Juſtice of His Majeſties Bench.	800	00	00
	Sir *Will. Aſton*, Kt. ſecond Juſtice of the ſaid Court.	300	00	00
	Thomas Stockton, Eſq; third Juſtice of the ſaid Court.	300	00	00
	Sir *Will. Uſher*, Kt. Clerk of the Crown, of the ſaid Court.	007	10	00
The Court of Chancery.	The moſt Reverend Father in God, *Michael* Lord Arch-biſhop of *Dublin*, Lord Chancellor of *Ireland*.	1000	00	00

Sir

	l.	s.	d.	
Sir *John Temple* Sen. Knt. Master of the *Rolls*.	144	03	04	The Court of Chancery.
Dr. *Dudley Loftus* one of the Masters of the *Chancery*.	020	00	00	
Robert Mossom, Esq; another Master of the *Chancery*.	020	00	00	
George Carlton Clerk of the Crown in *Chancery*.	025	00	00	
The said *George Carlton*, Clerk of the Hanaper, for his Fee *per Annum* 10 *l.* 10 *s.* and for an allowance of Paper and Parchment for the *Chancery*, *per Annum* 25 *l.* In all	035	10	00	
	1244	13	04	
Sir *Edward Smith*, Knt. Lord Chief Justice of the *Common-Pleas*.	600	00	00	The Court of *Common Pleas*.
Sir *Jerome Alexander*, Knt. Second Justice of the said Court.	300	00	00	
Robert Booth, Esq; Third Justice of the said Court.	300	00	00	
Sir *Walter Plunkett*, Knt. Prothonotary of the said Court.	007	10	00	
	1207	10	00	

Sir

		l.	*s.*	*d.*
Star-chamber.	Sir *George Lane*, Kn^t^. Clerk of the *Star-Chamber*.	010	00	00
	George Rutlidge, Marſhall of the *Star-chamber*.	010	00	00
		020	00	00
Officers attending the State.	Sir *Paul Davis*, Knt. Secretary of State, for his Fee	200	00	00
	The ſaid Sir *Paul Davis* for Intelligences	100	00	00
	The ſaid Sir *Paul*, Clerk of the Council, for his ancient Fee, *per Ann.* 7 *l.* 10 *s.* and for an Allowance for Paper and Parchment 40 *l.* in all	047	10	00
	Richard St. George, Eſq; *Ulſter* King at Arms	026	13	04
	Richard Carvy Athlong, Purſivant,	010	00	00
	Philip Carpinter, Eſq; Chief Serjeant at Arms, at 5 *s.* 6 *d.* *per diem*	100	07	06
	George Pigott, ſecond Serjeant at Arms for like Allowance	100	07	06
	George Wakefeild, Purſivant,	020	00	00
	William Roe, Purſivant,	020	00	00
	Arthur Padmor, Purſivant,	020	00	00

Thomas

	l.	*s.*	*d.*
Thomas Lee, Keeper of the Council-chamber.	018	05	00
Six Trumpeters and a Kettle-drum, at 60 *l.* each *per Ann.* 420. for their Fee, and 6 *l.* *per An.* each Board-wages 42 *l.* in all *per Ann.*	462	00	00
	1125	03	04

6 Trumpeters

Charge of Circuits.

The Chief, and other Justices of Assizes in every of the five Circuits twice a year, *per Annum*	1000	00	00
Robes for the Judges, *viz.* Three in the *Exchequer*, three in the *King's Bench*, three in the *Common-Pleas*, Master of the *Rolls*, and three of the King's Council, at 13 *l.* 6 *s.* 8 *d.* apiece *per Annum*, making in all	173	06	08

Liberates

Incidents.		l.	s.	d.
Incidents.	Liberates under the Seal of the *Exchequer* yearly, *viz.* the Chancellor of the *Exchequer* 13 *l.* 6 *s.* 8 *d.* the Chief Remembrancer 6 *l.* 13 *s.* 4 *d.* Clerk of the Pipe 6 *l.* 13 *s.* 4 *d.* the Usher 10 *l.* the Second Remembrancer 5 *l.* the Chief Chamberlain 5 *l.* the Second Chamberlain 5 *l.* Clerk of the *Common-Pleas* of the *Exchequer* 5 *l.* Summonister and Comptroller of the Pipe 5 *l.* The Customer at *Dublin* for Wax, Paper, Parchment and Ink 3 *l.* 15. *s.* in all *per Ann.*	082	01	08
	Rent of a House for the Receipts	025	00	00
	Keeper of the House for the Receipts	005	00	00
	Singers of *Christ-church* in *Dublin* for singing in the *Exchequer*, and praying for His Majesty, at 10 *s.* for every Term *per Ann.*	002	00	00
	Pursivants of the Exchequer for carrying Writs	071	05	00

Paper

	l.	s.	d.	
Paper and Parchments to the Courts	150	00	00	
The Nobility, Bishops and Councellors which shall reside and keep house in Ireland for impost of Wines, according to His Majesty's special grace				
	508	13	04	
	Besides impost of Wines.			
William Halsy, Esq; Chief Justice of the Province of *Munster*	100	00	04	Provincial Officers.
John Nayler, Second Justice of *Munster*	066	13	04	
Henry Batthurst, Attorney of the Province of *Munster*	013	06	08	
William Carr, Esq; Clerk of the Council of the said Province	007	10	00	
Walter Cooper, Serjeant at Arms there	020	00	00	
Oliver Jones, Chief Justice in the Province of *Connaght*	100	00	00	
Adam Cusack, Esq; second Justice of that Province	066	13	04	

John

		l.	s.	d.
	John Shadwell, Esq; Attorny for the said Province	020	00	00
	Sir *James Cuff*, Kn^t. Clerk of the Council there	007	10	00
	Thom. Elliot, Serjeant at Arms there	020	00	00

OFFICERS *of the Customs.*

		l.	s.	d.
Dublin.	*Thomas Worsop*, Esq; Customer of the Port of *Dublin*	007	10	00
	Will. Maul, Esq; Comptroller	007	10	00
	Will. Scott, Esq; Searcher	005	00	00
		020	00	00
Wexford.	*George Wakefeild*, Customer	010	00	00
	Hugh Poulder, Comptroller	005	00	00
		015	00	00
Waterford and *Ross.*	Sir *John Stephens*, Customer	015	00	00
	Frederick Christian, Comptroller	015	00	00
	Thom. Tint, Searcher	006	13	04
		036	13	04
Corke.	*Rich. Scudamore*, Customer	006	13	04
	Robert Williams, Searcher	005	00	00
		011	13	04

Robert

	l.	s.	d.	
Robert Southwell, Cuſtomer	13	06	08	*Kingſale.*
John Brown, Searcher	06	13	04	
	20	00	00	
John Selby, Cuſtomer	05	00	00	*Dingle. Icouſh.*
The Cuſtomer	13	06	08	*Limerick.*
Montfort Weſtrop Comptroller.	13	06	08	
John Lynch, Searcher.	05	00	00	
	31	13	04	
John Morgan, Cuſtomer.	13	06	08	*Galloway.*
The Searcher.	05	00	00	
	18	06	08	
Thomas Willis, Cuſtomer.	07	10	00	*Drogheda, Dundalk,* and *Carlingford.*
John Bulteele, Comptroller.	07	10	00	
Hugh Mountgomery, Searcher.	05	00	00	
	20	00	00	
Roger Lindon, Cuſtomer.	07	10	00	*Carrickfergus.*
Samuel Willby, Searcher.	06	13	04	
	14	03	04	
Nicholas Ward, Cuſtomer at *Strangford.*	07	10	00	*Strangford*

Robert

		l. s. d.
Newcastle, Dundrum, &c.	*Robert Hard*, Searcher at *Newcastle, Dundrum, Killaleagh, Bangor, Hollywood, Bellfast, Olderfleet, St. David, Whitehead, Ardglasse, Strangford, Ballintogher*, and *Donaghadee*.	06 13 04
The Office and Officers of the Excise	For the Salaries due to the Officers of the Excise.	4269 00 00
	The Contingent Charge of the Excise.	1200 00 00
		5469 00 00

These two Sums are to be distributed and apportioned as the Lord Lieutenant, or other Chief Governor, or Governors, and Council, shall think fit, the Custom and Excise being now Farm'd. These two Sums are to cease for the time of the Farm, and are not cast up in the Total.

Commissioner-General of the Customs and Excise. The said Commissioners, which are to be but five in number, are to have the allowance of one Penny in the pound each, for all Money to be received for Customs and Excise.

For

	l.	*s.*	*d.*	
For the Salaries of four Commiſſioners of Appeals in Cauſes of Exciſe, and New Impoſt. *viz.* Sir *James Ware*, Kt. *John Povey*, Eſq; Sir *William Uſher*, Kt. and *Peter Weybrants*, Alderman, at 150 *l.* a piece, *per Annum.*	600	00	00	Commiſſioners of Appeal.
Dr. *Robert Wood*, and *James Bonnell*, Accomptants General of the Cuſtoms and Exciſe, *per Annum.*	200	00	00	Accomptants-General of the Cuſtoms and Exciſe.
The Duke of *Ormond*	40	00	00	Creation-Money.
The Marquiſs of *Antrim*	40	00	00	
The Earl of *Caſtlehaven*	20	00	00	
The Earl of *Deſmond*	15	00	00	
The Earl of *Weſtmeath*	15	00	00	
The Earl of *Arglaſſe*	15	00	00	
The Earl of *Carbury*	15	00	00	
The Earl of *Cavan*	15	00	00	
The Earl of *Donnegale*	15	00	00	
The Earl of *Clanbrazill*	20	00	00	
The Earl of *Inchiquin*	20	00	00	
The Earl of *Orrery*	20	00	00	
The Earl of *Montrath*	20	00	00	
The Earl of *Tyrconnel*	20	00	00	

The

	l.	*s.*	*d.*
The Earl of *Clancarty*	20	00	00
The Earl of *Mount-Alexander*	20	00	00
The Earl of *Carlingford*	20	00	00
The Lord Viſcount *Grandiſon*	10	00	00
The Lord Viſcount *Willmot*	10	00	00
The Lord Viſcount *Valentia*	10	00	00
The Lord Viſcount *Dillon*	10	00	00
The Lord Viſcount *Nettervil*	10	00	00
The Lord Viſcount *Killulla*	10	00	00
The Lord Viſcount *Magennis*	10	00	00
The Lord Viſcount *Sarsfield* and *Kilmallake*	10	00	00
The Lord Viſcount *Ranelaugh*	10	00	00
The Lord Viſcount *Wenman* and *Tuam*	10	00	00
The Lord Viſcount *Shannon*	13	06	08
The Lord Viſcount *Clare*	10	00	00
The Lord Baron of *Cahir*	11	05	00
	484	11	08

Where Creation-Money is granted to one and the ſame Perſon for two Honours, that Sum which is granted with the higheſt Title, is only to be paid.

The

Perpetuities.

	l.	s.	d.
The Provost and Fellows of *Trinity-Colledge* near *Dublin*, by Patent, dated 12. *August*, 1612. as a perpetuity, *per Annum*..	388	15	00
The Dean and Chapter of *Christ-Church*, *Dublin*, grant in perpetuity, 12. *Junii*, 1604 *per Annum*.	045	06	08
The Lord Archbishop of *Dublin*, for Proxies due unto him out of divers Churches belonging to the late Monasteries of *Thomas Court*, St. *Maries* Abby, and St. *John* of *Jerusalem*, near *Dublin*, *per Annum*.	018	05	06
The Lord Bishop of *Meath* out of the Mannor of *Trim*.	003	15	00
The Mayor, Sheriffs, Commons, and Citizens of *Dublin*, *per Annum*.	500	00	00
The Chaunter of *Christ-Church*, *Dublin*, for the Rent of a Plat of Ground, near His Majesties Castle of *Dublin*.	027	00	00
	983	02	02

The

The Payments hereafter following, are to be continued to the present Grantees, during their Grants; but to cease afterwards, and not to be regranted, or paid to any other.

The most Reverend Father in God, *Michael* Lord Arch-Bishop of *Dublin*, Lord Chancellor of *Ireland*.	814	17	06
The Right Honourable *Richard* Earl of *Cork*, Treasurer.	365	00	00
Nicholas Loftus Esq;, Clerk of the Pipe.	025	00	00
Maurice Keating, Comptroller of the Pipe.	008	00	00
Sir *Theophilus Jones* Kt., Clerk of the Pells.	061	05	00
Bryan Jones Esq; Auditor of the Foreign Accompts and Prests, at 6 *s.* 8 *d. per diem* granted him by Letters Patents, dated 2. *April. Anno* 2*do. Caroli primi*, during his good behaviour, *per Annum.*	121	13	04

Edward

	l.	s.	d.
Edward Cook Esq;, one of the Masters of the *Chancery*.	020	00	00
John Westly Esq;, one of the Masters of the *Chancery*.	020	00	00
Anthony Walsh, Keeper of the Room, as also of the Robes, Hanging and Clock in the Castle of *Dublin* at 12 *d. per diem*.	018	05	00
John Crooke, Printer to His Majesty in *Ireland*.	008	00	00
Thomas Mall Esq;, Surveyor General of the Customs.	100	00	00
	1649	16	10

Temporary payments.

William Maule, Comptroller of the Customs at *Dublin*.	012	10	00
Marcus Viscount *Dungannon*, Master of the Game.	050	00	00
Sir *George Lane* Kt., for his Fee, as Keeper of the Records in *Brimingham's Tower*.	010	00	00
James Buck, Clerk of the Market of all *Ireland*.	020	00	00

The

	l.	*s.*	*d.*
The Counteſs of *Tyrconnell.*	300	00	00
Edward Fitz-Gerrald.	100	00	00
Sarah King, Widow.	080	00	00
Jane Cary, Widow.	050	00	00
John Dogharty at 18 *d. per diem.*	027	07	06
Jepſon Macguire.	040	00	00
Sir *Robert Meredith.*	100	00	00
Sir *George Blundell* at 6 *s. per diem.*	109	10	00
Ann Conocke.	050	00	00
William Awbry, at 1 *l. per* week.	052	00	00
Patrick Archer.	205	00	00

To be paid unto him until he be ſatiſfied the ſum of 5883 *l.* 19 *s.* 6 *d.* and 410 *l.* 5 *s.* 6 *d.* by Letters Patents dated 13 *March* 1662. and His Majeſties Letters of the 2*d* of *May* 1663.

Penſions and Annuities.

Dr. *John Sterne.*	060	00	00
Luke German Eſq;, *per annum*	100	00	00
Patrick Cowurcey, and his Son *John Cowurcey*, *per annum.*	150	00	00
Sir *James Dillon* per annum	500	00	00

Dr.

	l.	*s.*	*d.*
Dr. *Robert George*, per Annum	109	10	00
Thomas Piggot Esq;, per Annum	300	00	00
Mrs. *Mary Warren*, per Annum	080	00	00
Arthur Earl of *Anglesey*, per Annum	600	00	00
Captain *William Rosse*, per Annum	300	00	00
	3313	07	06

Commissioners of Accompts, for the yearly Accompts by them to be taken by virtue of His Majesty's Commission at 20 *l.* each of them *per Annum*, 220 *l.* And to the Clerks and others imployed in the said Accompts, 65 *l.* 10 *s.* In all,	285	10	00

Commissioners of Accompts and Clerks allowances.

For

Payments for extraordinaries by *Concordatum.*

	l. s. d.
For Fraught and Tranſportation, carrying of Letters and other Expreſſes, Gifts and Rewards, Sea-ſervice, Repairing and Upholding ſufficiently our Houſes, maintaining our Forts, finiſhing of needful undertakings of that kind, begun in other places, but not finiſhed; erecting of more ſtrengths of the like kind, and other fit and neceſſary places. Diets and Charges, in keeping of poor Priſoners, and ſick and maimed Soldiers in Hoſpitals; Printing, Riding and Travelling Charges; Preſts upon Accompt, and all other payments by Concordat of our Lieutenant, or other chief Governor or Governors, and Council, not to be exceeded without ſpecial direction firſt had from us, or our Privy-Council in *England*.	9000 00 00
Sum total of the payments aforeſaid upon the Civil Liſt amounts unto *per Annum*.	25601 4 8

Memo-

Memorandum. That the Impoſt of Wines, for the Nobility, Biſhops and Councillors, the Officers of the Exciſe, and Commiſſioners-general of the Cuſtoms and Exciſe, are not included in the abovesaid Sum.

AND Our Pleaſure is, That no Payment or Allowance be made by Concordat, but by Warrant drawn by the Clerk of the Council of Ireland, *and paſſed openly at our Council-Board there, and ſigned by our Lieutenant or other Chief-Governour, or Governour, Chancellor, Treaſurer, or Vice-Treaſurer, Chief-Baron and Secretary, or other four of them at the leaſt, the Lieutenant or Chief-Governour being one; and in default, either by exceeding the Sum limited by anticipation or otherwiſe, or by not obſerving of this our Direction and Commandment in every Point; Our Pleaſure is, That all Sums which ſhall otherwiſe be allowed and paid there, ſhall be ſet* inſuper, *as Debts upon our ſaid Lieutenant, or other Chief-Governour, or Governours; and our Under-Treaſurer, upon his Accounts to be defaulked to Our uſe, upon their ſeveral Entertainments.*

And

And Our further Pleaſure is, That this Eſtabliſhment and Liſt, containing all our Payments to be made for Civil-Cauſes, be duly paid according to our Directions, and be not exceeded, nor any of the Payments which are noted to be but temporary, or to ceaſe after Death, or ſurrender of the Party, or upon determination of his Grant, to be continued or renewed to any other, either in concurrence, reverſion or otherwiſe. And We require our Auditor-General, That once every Year, immediately upon the paſſing the Accounts of our Vice-Treaſurer, or Receiver General, a Tranſcript of the ſame Accompts, both for Receipts of every nature, and the particular Payments, be returned to our Treaſurer of England, *to the end we may be truly informed, both of the increaſe of our ſaid Revenues yearly, and alſo of the Abatements of Payments contained in this Liſt.*

ARLINGTON.

by

By the Lord-Lieutenant-General, and General Governor of *Ireland*.

I*Nstructions for our dearest Son,* Thomas *Earl of* Offory, *nominated by Us by virtue of His Majesty's Letters Patents, under His Great Seal of* England, *bearing date the* 21*st day of* February, *in the* 14*th Year of His Reign, and constituted by His Majesty's Letters Patents, under the Great Seal of this Kingdom of* Ireland, *bearing date the* 21*st day of* May, *in the* 16*th Year of His Reign, His Majesty's Deputy of this His said Kingdom, during His Majesty's Pleasure, and only in our Absence, until we shall return into this Kingdom.*

ORMOND.

W*Hereas We the Lord-Lieutenant received Instructions from the King's Most Excellent Majesty, under His Royal Signatures, bearing date the* 22*d day of* June, 1662. *We do herewith deliver you a Copy of the said Instructions signed by Us. And We do hereby require you to observe those Instructions, in all such Parts of them, as were to* be *be observed by Us, and are now appliable to you, in the Place of His Majesty's Deputy of this His Kingdom.*

You are to take care, That in your giving Commands, or Warrants for Payments of any of His Majesty's Treasure, or Moneys, you observe the Rule prescribed to you, in such Cases, by His Majesty's Letters Patents, whereby you are constituted His Majesty's Deputy of this His Kingdom.

Given at His Majesty's Castle of Dublin, *the 30th day of* May, 1664.

G. LANE.

The

The ***ESTABLISHMENT*** *and* ***LIST***; *Containing all the Payments to be made for Military Affairs in* Ireland, *to be duly paid by the Hands of our Vice-Treasurer, and Treasurer at Wars, according to the Cautions hereafter mentioned; the same to begin for and from the 1st Day of* April, 1666.

Signed, CHARLES *Rex*.

OFFICERS *General.*

	l. s. d.
THE Lord-Lieutenant and Governour-General of *Ireland*, for his Fee *per Ann. viz.* for his Diet, at 100 *l. per mensem*; a Retinue of 50 Horse, with Officers at 2 *l.* 19 *s.* 6 *d. per diem*; an Allowance of 1000 *l. per Ann.* in lieu of *cess*, an Allowance of 235 *l. per Ann.* in lieu of 235 Beefs, formerly paid to the Lord-Lieutenant, out of the County of *Cavan*; an Allowance of 240 *l. per Ann.* formerly paid to the Lord Lieutenant out of the Tythes of *Dunbogne*, making in all *per Ann.*	3860 17 06

As

LordLieutenant.

	l. s. d.
As General of the Army *per Ann.*	4331 06 08
As Capt. of a Troop of Horſe *per Ann.*	0723 18 04
As Collonel of Foot, *per Ann.*	0608 06 08
As Capt. of a Foot-Company, *per Ann.*	0261 11 08
	9786 00 10

For His Guard of Halberteers, conſiſting of a Capt. at 11 *l.* 4 *s.* each Calendar Month; a Lieutenant at 9 *l.* 16 *s.* two Serjeants at 3 *l.* 10 *s.* each; and 60 Halberteers at 2 *l.* 2 *s.* each, making *per Ann.*	1848 00 00
The Lieutenant-General of the Army at 1 *l. per diem.*	365 00 00

To Ceaſe *poſt mortem,* or other Determinations of the Grant made to *Thomas* Earl of *Oſſerey.*

The Serjeant Major-General of the Army, at 1 *l. per diem, per Ann.*	365 00 00

To

To Ceaſe *poſt mortem*, or other Determinations of the Grant made to *Roger* Earl of *Orery*.

	l.	s.	d.
Sir *Henry Titchburn*, K[t]. Marſhal of *Ireland*, for his Entertainment at 3 *s.* 9 *d. per diem*; a Trumpeter at 6 *d. ob q. per diem*, and a Retinue of 30 Horſe, at 9 *d.* a piece *per diem*, making *per Ann.*	489	06	07
The Commiſſary General of the Horſe, at 1 *l. per diem, per Ann.*	365	00	00

To Ceaſe *poſt mortem*, or other Determinations of the Grant, to *John* Lord *Kingſton*.

General Officers.

The Muſter-Maſter General, and Clerk of the Cheque, for his Entertainment, at 4 *s. per diem*, at 10 Horſe-Men, at 1 *s.* the piece *per diem*; for any encreaſe of his Entertainment 3 *s.* 6 *d. per diem*, with an Allowance for one Clerk at 2 *s.* 6 *d. per diem* making *per Ann.*	365	00	00
	3066	08	03

Six

	l.	s.	d.
Six Commissaries of the Musters, at 100 *per Ann.* each.	600	00	00
One Corporal of the Field, *viz.* Collonel *Beverly Usher,* at 5 *s. per diem; per Ann.*	091	05	00

To Ceafe *post mortem*, or other Determinations of the Grant in being.

The Advocate-General of the Army at 6 *s.* 8 *d. per diem.*	121	13	04
The Phyſician-General of the Army at 10 *s. per diem.*	182	10	00
Chirurgion of the Army in *Ireland*, and of the Hoſpital of *Dublin.*	121	13	04

OFFICERS Provincial.

	l.	s.	d.	q.
THE Lord Preſident of *Munſter*, for His Fee at 100 *l. Sterling per An.* for his Diet, and the Councils there, at 7 *l.* 10 *s. per* Week, and for his Retinue of 30 Horſe-Men, and 20 Foot-Men, at 1 *l.* 2 *s.* 6 *d. ob. per diem,* in all *per Annum.*	908	19	09	*ob.*

The

	l. s. d. q.
The Lord President of *Connaught*, for his Fee at 100 *l.* *Sterling per Ann.* for his Diet, and the Councils there, at 7 *l.* 10 *s. per* Week, and for his Retinue of 30 Horse-Men, and 20 Foot-Men, at 1 *l.* 2 *s.* 6 *d.* *ob per diem*, in all *per Ann.*	908 19 09 *ob.*
The Provost-Marshal of *Lemster*, for His Entertainment at 4 *s.* 2 *d. ob. q. per diem*, making *per Ann.*	077 03 07 *ob.*
	2126 14 02 *ob.*

Provincial Officers.

The Provost-Marshal of *Munster*, for his Entertainment at 4 *s.* 2 *d. ob q. per diem*, making *per Ann.*	077 03 07 *ob.*
The Provost-Marshal of *Connaught*, for his Entertainment, at 4 *s.* 2 *d. ob. q. per diem*, making *per Ann.*	077 03 07 *ob.*
The Provost Marshal of *Ulster*, for his Entertainment at 4 *s.* 2*d. ob. q. per diem*, making *per Ann.*	077 03 07 *ob.*

All

All the ſaid Provoſt-Marſhals, with the Entertainment due unto them reſpectively, to ceaſe *poſt mortem*, or other Determinations of their Grants.

CONSTABLES.

	l. *s.* *d.* *q.*
The Conſtable of *Dublin*-Caſtle, for his Entertainment at 20 *l. per Ann.*	020 00 00
The Porter of *Dublin*-Caſtle at 9 *d. per diem, per ann.*	013 13 09
The Conſtable of *Limerick*-Caſtle, for his Entertainment, at 10 *l. per ann.* and a Porter at 6 *d. ob q per diem, per ann.*	018 07 09 *ob.*
The Conſtable of *Athlone-Caſtle*, for his Entertainment, at 8*l.* 2*s.* 6 *d. per ann,* and a Porter at 6 *d. ob q. per diem, per ann.*	018 07 09 *ob.*
The Conſtable of *Roſcomon-Caſtle*, for his Entertainment, at 3 *s.* 4 *d. per diem.*	060 16 08
The Conſtable of *Carrickfergus*, for his Entertainment, at 2 *s.* 6 *d. per diem, per ann.*	045 12 06
	178 06 00 *ob.*

The

The Master of the Ordnance, with other Officers thereunto belonging, and Train of Artillery.

	l.	s.	d.
The Master of the Ordnance, for himself at 6 *s.* 8 *d.* *per diem*; a Lieutenant at 1 *s.* 6 *d.* *per diem*; a Cornet a 9 *d.* and 18 Horsemen at 1 *s.* the piece *per diem, per an.*	491	04	07
The Lieutenant of the Ordnance, at 7 *s.* *per diem, per an.*	127	15	00

To cease after the death of *Albert Cunningham*, now Patentee, or other determination of his Grant.

Officers of the Ordnance.

The Ingineer, Overseer, Surveyor, and Director-General of His Majesties Fortifications, *&c.* at 5 *s.* *per diem, per annum*	091	05	00

To cease after the death of Captain *John Payne* and Capt. *John Hallam*, now Patentees, or other determinations of their Grant.

Captain *Hugh Magill*, Comptroller of the Ordnance, for his Fee, at 5 *s.* *per diem*, and for an allowance of 1 *s.* *per diem* for his Clerk, both *per annum.*	109	10	00
	819	14	07

Sundry

Sundry Ministers belonging to the Ordnance, viz. *in*

LEMSTER.

	l.	*s.*	*d.*
A Master-Gunner at 3 *s.* *per diem*, his Mate at 1 *s.* 6 *d.* *per diem*; six Gunners for the Train, at 1 *s.* 2 *d.* each *per diem*; one Gentleman of the Ordnance at 3 *s.* *per diem*; Clerk of the Ordnance and Stores at *Dublin* at 4 *s.* *per diem*, his Clerk at 1 *s.* *per diem*; Gunsmith, Blacksmith, Carpenter and Wheeler, at 1 *s.* 4 *d.* *per diem* each, Armorer, Cutler, Cooper, at 9 *d.* each *per diem*; six Matrosses at 8 *d.* each *per diem*; three Waggoners at 10 *d.* each *per diem*; at *Duncannon*, a Clerk of the Stores 1 *s.* 8 *d.* *per diem*, a Gunner at 1 *s.* *per diem*, a Matross, at 8 *d.* *per diem*; at *Passage*, a Gunners-Mate at 10 *d.* *per diem*; making *per annum*	774	02	01

CON-

CONNAUGHT.

	l.	s.	d.
At *Athlone*, a Clerk of the Stores at 1 *s.* 8 *d. per diem*; a Gunner at 1 *s. per diem*; a Matroſs at 8 *d. per diem. Galloway*, a Clerk of the Stores at 1 *s.* 8 *d. per diem*; a Gunner at 1 *s. per diem*; a Matroſs at 8 *d. per diem.* At *Sligo*, a Gunner at 1 *s. per diem*; Iſle of *Arran*, a Gunner at 1 *s. per diem*; *Inniſbuffin*, a Gunner at 1 *s. per diem*; making *per annum*,	176	08	04

MUNSTER.

MVNSTER.

Ministers belonging to the Ordnance.		l.	s.	d.
	Waterford, a Gunner at 1 *s. per diem*; a Matroſs at 8 *d. per diem*. *Limerick*, a Clerk of the Stores at 1 *s.* 8 *d. per diem*; a Gunner at 1 *s. per diem*; a Matroſs at 8 *d. per diem*. *Cork*, Clerk of the Stores at 1 *s.* 8 *d. per diem*; a Gunner at 1 *s. per diem*; a Matroſs at 8 *d. per diem*. At *Halvowling*, a Gunners-Mate 10 *d. per diem*; *Youghall*, a Gunner, at 1 *s. per diem*; *Kingſale*, a Gunner, at 1 *s. per diem*; at the Block-houſe, a Gunners-Mate, at 10 *d. per diem*; at *Crook-haven*, a Gunner, at 1 *s. per diem*; at *Inniſherkin*, a Gunners Mate, at 10 *d. per diem*; *Valentia*, a Gunner, at 1 *s. per diem*; in all *per annum*.	270	14	02
		1358	02	10

VLSTER.

ULSTER.	*l.*	*s.*	*d.*
Londonderry, a Clerk of the Stores, at 1 *s.* 8 *d. per diem*; a Gunner, at 1 *s. per diem*; a Matross, at 8 *d. per diem.* At *Culmore*, a Gunners-mate at 10 *d. per diem.* At *Carrickfergus*, a Clerk of the Stores, at 1 *s.* 8 *d. per diem*; a Gunner at 1 *s.*; a Matross at 8 *d. per diem.* In all, *per annum*	136	17	06
	HORSE.		
The King's Guard of Horse consisting of a Captain at 19 *l.* 12 *s.* each Calendar Month; a Lieutenant at 12 *l.* 12 *s.*; a Cornet at 12 *l.* 12 *s.*; a Quartermaster at 9 *l.* 16 *s.*; six Corporals at 6 *l.* 6 *s.* each; two of the King's Trumpets at 6 *l.* 6 *s.* each; four more of the King's Trumpets, and a Kettle-drum at 3 *l.* 10 *s.* each, besides their standing-allowances in the Civil List: A Sadler, Farrier, and Armorer, at 4 *l.* 18 *s.* each; and 100 Horsemen at 4 *l.* 18 *s.* each making in all *per mens.* 627 *l.* 4 *s.* which amounts for the whole Pay of the said Guard *per An.* unto	7526	8	

2 + 4 Trumpets
4
Kettle-drum

The

	l.	s.	d.
The Lord Lieutenant's Troop, consisting of a Captain at 19 *l.* 12 *s.* each Calendar Month; a Lieutenant at 12 *l.* 12 *s.* and a Cornet at 9 *l.* 16 *s.*; a Quarter-master at 7 *l.* three Corporals and two Trumpets more at 6 *l.* 6 *s.* each; and fifty private Horsemen at 2 *l.* 2 *s.* each; making in all *per mens.* 184 *l.* 2 *s.* which amounts for the whole Pay of the said Troop *per an.* unto	2209	4	
Five Troops more belonging to the General Officers, *viz.* to the Lieutenant General of the Army, the Serjeant Major General of the Army, the Lord President of *Connaught*, the Commissary General of the Horse, and the Scoutmaster-General of the Army, each Troop consisting of a Captain at 19 *l.* 12 *s.* each Calendar Month, a Lieutenant at 12 *l.* 12 *s.* a Cornet at 9 *l.* 16 *s.* a Quarter-master	10290		

	l.	s.	d.
Master at 7 *l.* Three Corporals, and two Trumpets at 3 *l.* 10*s.* each, and 50 private Horsemen, at 2*l.* 2.*s.* each making in all *per mensem* for each Troop, 171 *l.* 10 *s.* which amounts for the whole pay of the said five Troops *per annum* unto	1226	8	
Twenty three Troops, which consisting of the like Officers, and forty five private Horsemen, making in all *per mensem* to each Troop 161 *l.* whic amounts for the whole pay of the said twenty three Troops *per annum* unto	44436		

2 Trumpeters

FOOT.

The Lord Lieutenant's Company, consisting of a Captain at 11 *l.* 4 *s.* each Callendar Month. A Lieutenant at 5 *l.* 12 *s.* an Ensign at 4 *l.* 4 *s.* Two Serjeants at 2 *l.* 2 *s.* each; three Corporals and two Drums at 1 *l.* 8 *s.* each, and one hundred private Footmen at 14 *s.* each, making in all			

2 Drums

per

	l.	*s.*	*d.*
per mensem 102 *l.* 4 *s.* which amounts for the whole pay of the said Company *per annum* unto	1226	8	0
Fifty nine Companies more, each consisting of a Captain at 11 *l.* 4 *s.* each Calender Month, a Lieutenant at 5 *l.* 12 *s.* an Ensign at 4 *l.* 4 *s.* two Serjeants at 2 *l.* 2 *s.* each; three Corporals, and one Drummer at 1 *l.* 8 *s.* each, and sixty private Footmen at 14 *s.* each, making in all *per mensem* for each Company 72 *l.* 16 *s.* which amounts for the whole pay of the said fifty nine Companies *per annum* unto	51542	0	8
A Ward at *Sligo* under the command of Major *Robert Edgeworth* consisting of two Serjeants at 2 *l.* 2 *s.* each, every Calender Month; three Corporals, and one Drummer at 1 *l.* 8 *s.* each, and sixty private Footmen, at 14 *s.* each; making in all *per mensem* 51 *l.* 16 *s.* which amounts *per annum* unto	0621	12	
	53390	8	

Regi-

Regiment of Guards.

	l.	s.	d.
The Royal Regiment of Guards, consisting of twelve Companies, *viz.* a Colonel as Colonel and Captain at 28 *l. per mensem* a Lieutenant-Colonel, and Captain at 21 *l. per mensem.* A Major and Captain at 16 *l.* 16 *s.* Nine Captains more at 11 *l.* 4 *s.* each; twelve Lieutenants at 5 *l.* 12 *s.* each; twelve Ensignes at 4 *l.* 4 *s.* each; forty Serjeants at 2 *l.* 2 *s.* each; thirty six Corporals at 1 *l.* 8 *s.* each; Drum-Major at 2 *l.* 16 *s.* Twenty four Drummers at 1 *l.* 8 *s.* each; a Piper to the Kings Company at 1 *l.* 8 *s.* Twelve hundred Soldiers at 1 *l.* 3 *s.* 4. *d.* each; a Chaplain at 9 *l.* 6 *s.* 8 *d.* An Adjutant, Quarter-Master, and Chyrurgeon at 5 *l.* 12 *s.* each, and Chirurgeons Mate at 3 *l.* 10 *s.* making in all *per mens.* at 28 days to the Month 1886 *l.* 00. 08. which amounts unto *per annum*	24518	8	8

24 Drummers + Piper

Tempo-

	l.	*s.*	*d.*

Temporary Payments.

Sir *Henry Titchburn*, Knight, Marſhall of *Ireland*,	198	1	9

To ceaſe Poſt-mortem *or other Determination of his Grant.*

Sir *Theophilus Jones*, Scout-maſter General of the Army, for his Entertainment at 6 *s.* 8 *d. per diem*, and for an encreaſe of his Entertainment at 100 *l. per annum* making in all	221	13	4

To ceaſe Poſt-mortem *or other Determination of his Grant.*

Sir *George Lane* Knight, for his Entertainment as Secretary at War to his Majeſty, at 1 *l. per diem* for himſelf, and 5 *s. per diem* for his Clerk *per annum*	456	5	0

To ceaſe Poſt-mortem, *or other Determination of his Grant.*

Cap.

	l.	s.	d.
Captain *Richard St.George* the pay of a Captain of Foot towards his maintenance during his life being 11 *l.* 4 *s.* *per mensem*; *per annum*	134	8	
Arthur Earl of *Donnegall* for his Entertainmont at 4 *s.* 2 *d.* *per diem* for himself and for nine Horsemen at 9 *d.* each *per diem* during his life, by vertue of a Grant thereof, dated the last of *July* in the 13*th*. year of King *James*, *per ann.*	199	4	7
The Mayor of the City of *Dublin* for his Entertainment at 8 *s.* *per diem*	146		
	2255	9	4

Particular Governours.

The Governour of the County of *Clare* for his Fee at 10 *s.* *per diem*; *per annum*	182	10
The Governour of the Castle of *Dublin* for his Fee 1 *l.* *per diem*; *per annum*	365	

The

	l.	s.	d.
The Governour of the Fort of *Sligo* for his Fee at 10 *s. per diem*; *per annum*	182	10	
The Governour of the Fort of *Halbolling* for his Fee at 6 *s. per diem*; *per annum*	109	10	
The Constable of *Hilsborough* at 3 *s.* 4 *d. per diem*; *per annum*	060	16	8

These Temporary Payments to cease Post mortem, *or other determination of the said Grants, except that of the* Halboling.

Sum total of the payments aforesaid upon the Military List amounts unto *per ann.*

l.	s.	d.	ob.
163810	3	11	

By His Majesties Command,

ARLINGTON.

A

A Catalogue of the *PEERS*.

Duke of *Ormond*
Duke of *Leinster*
Marquess of *Antrim*

EARLS.

Kildare
Thomond
Cork
Desmond
Barrymore
Meath
Ossory
Roscommon
Londonderry
Donnigall
Arran
Conaway
Carberry
Ardglass
Rannalagh
Cavan
Inchiquin
Clancarty
Orrery
Mamtroth
Drogheda
Waterford
Mount-Alexander
Down
Longford
Tyrone
Bellomont.
Clanrickard
Castlehaven
Westmeath
Fingall
Castlemaine
Carlingford

Viscounts.

Grandison
Wilmot
Loftus of Ely
Swords
Kilmurry
Valentia
Mareborough

Castleton

Castleton
Chaworth
Sligo
Waterford
Strangford
Tuam
Cashell
Carlo
Cullen
Shannon
Mazareene
Dromoor
Dungarvan
Dungannon
Kells
Fitzharding
Clare
Charlemount
Powerscourt
Blesington
Granard
Lansborough
Ross.

Castalo
Merrion
Fairfax
Fitz-Williams
Gormanston
Rathcoole
Barefore
Brucher
Galmoy
Kingsland
Mountgarret
Douth
Evagh
Killmallock
Ikernie
Glanmalegra
Claine
Downe
Trazey.

Archbishopricks and Bishopricks in *Ireland.*

ARchbishoprick of *Armagh*
—— —— *Dublin*
—— —— —— *Cashells*

Arch-

Archbiſhop. of *Tuam*
Biſhoprick of——
——*Meath*
——*Kildore*
——*VVaterford*
——*Clonfert*
——*Elphin*
— *Fernes & Laghlin*
——*Clogher*
——*Dromore*
——*Oſſory*
——*Derry*
——*Down*
——*Killallow*
——*Cork*
——*Limerick*
——*Cloyne*
——*Killalla*
——*Rapho*
——*Kilmore*

BARONS.

Kingſale
Kerry
Hoath
Mountjoy
Folliot
Maynard

Barons.

Dundalk
Digby
Lifford
Herbert
Lochlin
Colraine
Leitrim
Donamore
Blare
Killard
Kingſton
Colooney
Sautrey
Lough
Glawnalley
Caſtle-Steward

Atheury
Caſhir
Baltimore
Strabane
Slane
Trimleſton
Dunſcany
Dunboyne
Upper Oſſery
Caſtle-Comell
Brittas

A

A List of thoſe Places that return Parliament Men in *Ireland*

Leinſter.

County of Catherlough 2
Burrough of Catherlough 2
B. of Old-Leighlen 2

County of Dublin 2
City of Dublin 2
University *of* Dublin 3
Bur. of Newcaſtle 2
B. of Swords 2

Village de Drogheda 2

County of Kilkenny 2
Bur. of Callen 2
B. of Thomas-Town 2
B of Gowran 2
B. of Kells 2
B. of Emiſteogue 2
B. of Knoctopher 2
B. of St. Kennis 2
City of Kilkenny 2

County of Kildare 2
Bur. of Kildare 2
B. of Naſs 2
B. of Athy 2

Com. Regis 2
Bur. of Phillipps-Town 2
B. of Byrr 2
B of Banagher 2

County of Meath 2
Bur. of Trim 2
B. of Kells 2
B. of Navan 2
B. of Athbuy 2
B. of Duleeke 2
B. of Ratooth 2

Com. Regine 2
Bur. of Bellakill 2
B. of Mariborough 2
Port Arlinton 2

County

County of West-meath 2
Bur. of Athlone 2
B. of Fower 2
B. of Kilbegan 2
B. of Mullingar 2

County of Wicklow 2
Bur. of Wicklow 2
B. of Carisford 2
B. of Baltinglass 2

County of Wexford 2
Town of Wexford 2
Town of Ross 2
Bur. of Eniscourthy 2
B. of Featherd 2
B. of Bannow 2
B. of Cloghmaine 2
B. of Arkloe 2
B. of Taughman 2
B. of Newburrough 2

County of Longford 2
Burrough of Lanisbo-rough 2

County of Louth 2
Bur. of Dundalke 2
B. of Arthdee 2
B. of Carlingford 2

Munster.

County of Cork 2
City of Cork 2
Burrough of Mallow 2
B. of Baltimore 2
B. of Clognekilty 2
B. of Bandonbridge 2
B. of Kingsaile 2
B. of Youghall 2

County of Clare 2
Bur. of Insh 2

County of Kerry 2
Bur. of Traly 2
B. of Dinglecough 2
B. of Ardfart 2

County of Limerick 2
City of Limerick 2
Bur. of Kilmallock 2
B. of Askaton 2

County of Tippera-ry 2

Town

Town of Tipperary 2
Bur. of Clonmell 2
B. of Feathard 2
Town of Cashell 2
B. of Thurles 2

County of Water-ford 2
City of Waterford 2
Bur. of Dungarvan 2
B. of Lismore 2
B. of Tallow 2

Ulster.

County of Armagh 2
Burrough of Ar-magh 2
B. of Charlemont 2

Connty of Antrim 2
Bur. of Belfast 2
B. of Carickfergus 2
B. of Lisborne 2
B. of Antrim 2

County of Cavan 2
Bur. of Cavan 2
B. of Bellturbet. 2

County of Down 2
Bur. of Down 2
B. of Newtown 2
B. of Newry 2
Ballkillaleagh 2
B. of Bangor 2
B. of Hilsburough 2

County of Donne-gal 2
Bur. of Lifford 2
B. of Ballishannon 2
B. of Kilbegs 2
B. of Donnigall 2
Bur. of St. John's-Town 2

County of Far-manaugh 2
Bur. of Inniskilling 2

County of London-derry 2
City of Londonder-ry. 2
Bur. of Colerain 2
B. of Lanmevaddy 2
County of Mona-ghan 2

Bur.

Bur. of Monaghan	2	*Bur. of* Carickdrum-rusk	2
County of Tyrone	2		
Bur. of Donnegall	2	*County of* Mayo	2
Town of Clogher	2	*Bur. of* Caſtle-Bar	2
Bur. of Agber	2		
B. of Strabaine	2	*County of* Roſcomon	2
Connaught.		*Bur. of* Roſcomon	2
		B. of Tulsk	2
County of Galloway	2		
Bur. of Gall way	2	*County of* Sligo	2
B. of Athenry	2	*Bur. of* Sligo	2
B. of Tuam	2		
County of Leitrim	2	*The whole Number.*	285.
Bur. of James-Town	2		

VER-

VERBUM SAPIENTI.

VERBUM SAPIENTI.

THE INTRODUCTION.

1 WHEREAS many are forced to pay $\frac{1}{10}$ of their whole Estates towards the raising of but 70000 *l.* *per Mensem*, besides what they pay more insensibly and directly, as Customs, Excise, Chimny-Money, *&c.* (*viz.* in *London*, they pay 2*d.* *per Mensem per* Pound Rent, that is 2 *s.* *per Annum*, or $\frac{1}{10}$ of the whole.) It must come to pass, that the same Persons must from *Christmas*, 1665. pay $\frac{1}{3}$ of their whole Estates, if the War with *Holland* continue two years longer, at the value of the last years Expence, provided His Majesty be kept out of Debt.

2. But

2. But if the Publick Charge were laid proportionably, no Man need pay above $\frac{1}{10}$ of his whole Effects, even in case the Tax should rise to 250 000 *l. per Mensem*, which God forbid.

3. That is to say, according to the present ways, some pay four times as much more as they ought, or needed; which disproportion is the true and proper Grievance of Taxes, and which must be felt when the Tax happens to be great and extraordinary: Whereas by meer Method and Proportion, the same may be corrected as aforesaid; and withal, just Accounts might be kept of the People, with the respective Increases and Decreases of them their Wealth, and Foreign Trade.

CHAP.

CHAP. I.

Containing several Computations of the Wealth of the Kingdom.

1. THERE are of Men, Women, and Children, in *England* and *Wales*, about six Millions, whose Expence at 6 *l.* 13 *s.* 4 *d.* *per Annum*, or near 4½ *d.* *per Diem*, for Food, Housing, Cloaths, and all other necessaries, amount to 40 Millions, *per Annum*.

2. There are in *England* and *Wales*, of Acres of Land (worth 6 *l.* 1 *s.* 8 *d.* *per* Acre, and 18 years purchase) 24 Millions, that is, which yields 8 Millions *per Annum* Rent, and which are worth 144 Millions to be sold.

3. There be 28000 Houses within the Liberties of the City of *London*, worth 15 *l.* *per Annum*, and twelve years purchase (*viz.* which yield 420,000 *l.* *per Annum*, and are worth 5,040000 *l.*

(*viz.*

There are without the Liberties, but within the Bills of Mortality $\frac{1}{4}$ more in number, perhaps not of greater value, *viz.* 5,040000 *l.*

4. There is in all *England* and *VVales* near ten times as many Chimneys as within the Liberties of *London*, as appears by the Returns; Whereof those within the Bills are $\frac{1}{5}$ of the whole.

5. 'Tis probable, that the Housing of all the Cities and Market-Towns, are double in number to those of all *London*, though of no more worth.

6. 'Tis also probable, that the Housing without the Cities and Towns, are more in number than those within (*London* excepted) but of no more value.

7. So as the Housing of *England* may be estimated worth 30 millions; and that if their values be estimated by Chimneys, those of *London* are worth 12 *d.* *per* Chimney; those in the Suburbs 10 *d.* other Cities and Market-Towns 6 *d.* and those without both, about 4 *d.*

8. The Shipping of *England*, &c. is about 500000 Tuns, which at 6 *d.* *per* Tun, including their Ordnance, Apparel, &c. is worth three millions.

9. The

9. The Stock of Cattel on the aforementioned 24 millions of Land, and the Waſte thereunto belonging, is worth $\frac{1}{4}$ of the ſaid Land, *viz.* 36 millions comprehending Horſes, Oxen, Sheep, Swine, Deer, Fiſheries, Parks and Warrens.

10. The Coined Gold and Silver of the Kingdom, is ſcarce worth ſix millions.

11. The Wares, Merchandizes, and Utenſils of Plate, and Furnitures, may be eſtimated at 31 millions to make the Ships and Money 40. and the whole 250 millions.

12. The moſt uncertain part of this Eſtimate, ſeems to be rating perſonal Eſtates at above 30 Millions, which I make probable thus.

(1) Firſt it is not unlikely that what is contained in all the Shops, Warehouſes, Cellars, Barns, and Graineries, together with Houſehold Furniture, Cloaths, Ornaments, *&c.* ſhould be leſs worth than Houſing it ſelf that contains them.

(2) If the value of all the Cattel, *viz.* 36 millions, were added to the 31 perſonal Eſtates, making 67 together; both will not make up $1\frac{3}{4}$ years Proviſion for the whole Nation, whoſe Expence we eſtimated at 40 millions *per annum*; and poorer than ſo, we hope it is not.

(3.) I

(3.) I find by the particular eſtimate of the values of all the Plate, Lead, Iron, Copper and Tin, and of all the Timber, Planks, and Woods, and of all Silks, Linnen, and Callicoes; of all Clothes, Stuffs, and Leathers; of all Grains, and Salts, and of all Wines, Oyles, and other Liquids; of all Grocery and Spicery, and Drugs; of Jewels, and Hangings, Beds, and other Ornaments, (too troubleſome to particularize) that this general Account may ſtand.

(4.) The City of *London* being commonly eſteemed and rated at the 15*th* part of the whole, which we reckon at 250 Millions, that is 16$\frac{2}{3}$. I think the ſum may be well made up by reckoning 5$\frac{1}{6}$ Millions for the Houſing as aforeſaid, and 1$\frac{1}{2}$ for the Shipping (half the Shipping of the Nation belonging to *London*) and about the double of the value of the Houſing for what is contained in them. The which upon conſidering many ſeveral Houſes, I find not unreaſonable.

(Laſtly,) ſuppoſing that in the Houſes within the Liberties of *London* (worth 5 Millions) there be 10 Millions worth of Goods; I conceive that to allow about as much more, *viz.* 21 Millions) to all the reſt of the Houſes in the Kingdom, which are ten times as many as aforeſaid, will not overcharge them.

13. Now

13. Now if the Land worth 144 Millions, yield 8 Millions *per annum*, the other Estate converted into the like Species must yield $5\frac{8}{9}$ more; but because Money and other personal Estates yield more *per annum* than Land; (that is) doubles it self under 17 years purchase at 6 *l. per centum*, then instead of $5\frac{8}{9}$, suppose it to yield 7, making the whole Annual Proceed 15.

CHAP. II.

Of the Value of the PEOPLE.

NOW if the Annual proceed of the Stock, or Wealth of the Nation, yields but 15 millions, and the expence be 40. Then the labour of the People must furnish the other 25; which may be done, if but half of them, *viz.* 3 millions earned but 8 *l.* 6 *s.* 8 *d. per annum*, which is done at 7 *d. per diem*, abating the 52 Sundays, and half as many other days for accidents as Holy days, sickness, recreations, *&c.*

2. If $\frac{1}{6}$ of these 3 millions earned but 2 *d. per diem*; another $\frac{1}{6}$ 4 *d.* another $\frac{1}{6}$ 8 *d. per diem*, another 10 *d.* and another 12 *d.* The medium will be this, 7 *d. per diem.*

3. Where-

3. Whereas the Stock of the Kingdom, yielding but 15 Millions of proceed, is worth 250 Millions; then the People who yield 25, are worth $416\frac{2}{3}$ Millions. For although the Individiums of Mankind be reckoned at about 8 years purchaſe; the Species of them is worth as many as Land, being in its nature as perpetual, for ought we know.

4. If 6 Millions of People be worth 417 millions of pounds *Sterling*, then each head is worth 69 *l.* or each of the 3 millions of Workers is worth 138 *l.* which is 7 years purchaſe, at about 12 *d. per diem*; nor is ſuperlucration above his ſubſiſtence to be reckoned in this Caſe.

5. From whence it follows, that 100,000. perſons dying of the Plague, above the ordinary number, is near 7 Millions loſs to the Kingdom; and conſequently how well might 70,000 *l.* have been beſtowed in preventing this Centuple loſs?

6. We ſaid, that the late mortality by the Peſt, is a great loſs to the Kingdom; whereas ſome think it but a ſeaſonable diſcharge of its Peſtilent humours: to clear which difficulty, I ſay,

7. If the Plague diſcerned well, between the well and the ill-affected to Peace and Obedience,

dience, or between the *Bees* and the *Drones*, the Fact would determine the Question: But if it destroy promiscuously, the Loss is proportionable to the Benefit we have by them that survive; for 'tis they that make *England* worth above 600 millions, as aforesaid: It being certain, That if one person only had escaped; the whole Territory, and all that is in it, had been worth but a livelihood for that one; and he subject to be a prey to the next two that should invade him.

8. It seems reasonable, that what we call the Wealth, Stock, or Provision of the Nation, being the effect of the former or past labour, should not be conceived to differ from efficiencies in being, but should be rated alike, and contribute alike to the common necessities: And then of all and every summ to be raised, the Land and Stock must pay 3 parts; and the People considered without any Estate at all, 5 more; the whole into 8 divided.

9. If the expence of the Nation be 40 Millions; it seems but the same hardship to set apart 4. *viz.* $\frac{1}{10}$ of the whole for the publick use, as what now lies upon many already: But 4 Millions would afford one for the ordinary Expence, and three

three for the extraordinary Wars, that is 250 000 *l. per mensem*; that is $3\frac{1}{2}$ as much as 70. For the raising whereof, many now pay above a $\frac{1}{10}$ of their whole Estates, for want of Method and Proportion.

10. Labouring men work 10 hours *per diem*, and make 20 meals *per* week, *viz.* 3 a day for working-days, and two on *Sundays*; whereby it is plain, that if they could fast on *Fryday* nights, and Dine in one hour and an half, whereas they take two, from eleven to one; thereby this working $\frac{1}{20}$ more, and spending $\frac{1}{20}$ less, the $\frac{1}{10}$ abovementioned might be raised, at least with more ease, than to take up Arms, and resist it.

CHAP. III.

Of the several Expences of the Kingdom, and its Revenues.

THE ordinary Expence of the Kingdom for the Navy, Ordnance, Garisons, Land-forces, *Tangier*, *Jamaica*, *Bombay*, Ambassadors, Pensions, Intelligence, Kings and Royal Families Expence, consisting of the Houshold, of the King,

King, Queen, Duke, *&c.* Privy-Purſe, Wardrobe, Robes, Angel-Gold, Maſter of the Horſe, Mews, Armory, Tents, Parks, Lodges, Goldſmiths, Jewels, *&c.* hath been computed to be about one Million; Reckoning 200 000 *l.* for the Navy, 60 for the Ordnance and Powder, 290 for Land-forces, Gariſons, *&c.* and 450 000 for other things.

2. Towards this, there is in Crown-Lands 70 080, Poſt-Office 20, Coynage and Pre-emption of Tinn 12, Foreſt of Deer 4, Courts of Juſtice 6, Firſt Fruits 18; in all 1,30 000. Cuſtoms at 2 *per Centum* 170. in all 300 000. without the Duties of Wares, Wine-Licence, Aulnage or Butlerage, Exciſe, Chimney-money, Land-tax, Pole and Aſſeſments, being regulated and proportionated as followeth: *viz.*

CHAP. IV.

Of the Method of apportioning Taxes.

1. IF a Million is to be raiſed above the 300 000 *l.* laſt mentioned, then 375 000 *l.* is to be levied on the Stock, and 625000 *l.* on the People.

Of

Of the 375,000.	on the Stock,	
	216	on the Lands,
	54	on the Cattel, &c.
	60	on the Personal Estates,
	45	on the Housing.
in all	375	

2. To raise 216,000 *l.* out of 8,000,000 *M.* Rent, requires $\frac{1}{37}$ of the Rent, and $\frac{1}{27}$ of $\frac{1}{37}$; but allowing the charge of Collecting, we may express it to a $\frac{1}{36}$ part.

3. To raise 54000 *l. per annum*, out of 36,000000 *M.* requires the annual payment of a 666th part of the whole value; but in regard of Charges, let it be reduced to a 600th part.

4. The like for the 60000 *l.* of Personal Estates.

5. To raise 45000 *l. per annum*, from all the Housing worth 30 *Millions*, or 7500 for the Housing in *London*-Liberties, worth about 5 *Millions*, and whose Rent is 4,20 000 *l. per annum*, requires but $\frac{1}{56}$ of the annual Rent, which cannot be above 12 *d.* a Chimney *per Annum*, reckoning 5 to each House. Without the Liberties, about 10 *d.* the Chimney will effect the same; 6 *d.* in the Cities and Market-Towns, and 4 *d.* elsewhere.

6. As

6. As for the 625, 000 *l.* to be raised by the People, it requires but 2 *s.* 1 *d. per* Pole *per Annum*, which let rather be divided into a Pole of 6 *d.* a Head, and an Excise of 19 *d.* which is not the full $\frac{1}{84}$ part of the mean expence, 6 *l.* 13 *s.* 4 *d.* so as the $\frac{11}{84}$ of the value of Consumptions, will with the said 6 *d.* Pole, raise 625, 000 *l. per Annum.*

CHAP. V.

Of Money; and how much is necessary to drive the Trade of the Nation.

1. IT may be asked, If there were occasion to raise 4 *Millions per Annum*, whether the same 6 *Millions* (which we hope we have) would suffice for such revolutions and circulations thereof as Trade requires? I answer yes; for the Expence being 40 Millions, if the revolutions were in such short Circles, *viz.* weekly, as happens among poor Artizans and Labourers, who receive and pay every *Saturday*, then $\frac{40}{52}$ parts of 1 Million of Money would answer those ends: But if the Circles be quarterly, according to our Custom of paying rent, and gathering Taxes, then 10 Millions were requisite. Wherefore supposing payments in general to be of a mixt Circle between One week

week and 13. then add 10 Millions to $\frac{10}{32}$, the half of the which will be $5\frac{1}{2}$, ſo as if we have $5\frac{1}{2}$ Millions, we have enough.

2. And thus I have ſhewed, That if one half of the Subjects of *England* (playing 78 days in the year) will earn 7 *d. per diem* all the reſt of the days one with another; And if they would work $\frac{1}{20}$ more, and ſpend $\frac{1}{20}$ leſs, they might enable their King to maintain double the Forces he now doth, without ſuffering in the general more than many well affected perſons do now through negligence, or miſtakes in their Particulars. Nor is Money wanting to anſwer all the Ends of a well Policed State, notwithſtanding the great decreaſes thereof, which have happened within theſe Twenty Years.

Nor were it hard to ſubſtitute in the place of Money (were a competency of it wanting) what ſhould be equivalent unto it. For Money is but the Fat of the Body-Politick, whereof too much doth as often hinder its Agility, as too little makes it ſick. 'Tis true, that as Fat lubricates the motion of the Muſcles, feeds in want of Victuals, fills up uneven Cavities, and beautifies the Body; ſo doth Money in the State quicken its Action, feeds from abroad in time of Dearth at home; evens accounts by reaſon of of it's divisibility, and beautifies the whole, altho more especially the particular persons that have it in plenty.

CHAP. VI.

The Causes of irregular Taxing.

1. THE Causes of Error in this great Affair of Publick Levies, have been these. First, Laying too great a stress on the matter of Money, which is to the whole effect of the Kingdom but as 6 to 667. That is, not one to 100. Secondly, Laying the whole Burthen on the past Effects, and neglecting the present Efficiencies, exceeding the former as 417 doth 250. Thirdly, Reckoning all the personal Estates of the City of *London* (Shipping included) at scarce ½ the value of the very Housing, whereas they are double: Which happens because the Housing of *London* belongs to the Church, Companies, or Gentlemen, and are taxed by the Citizens their Tenants. Fourthly, A fallacious tenderness towards the poor, (who now pay scarce 1 *s. per* head *per ann.* towards all manner of charges) interwoven with the cruelty of not provi-

providing them Work, and indulging Laziness in them, because of our own indisposition to employ them; so some are over-charged through evil Custom, and others left to sordid Want, and bruitish Irregularity. Fifthly, An Opinion, that certainty of Rules is impossible, and but an idle Notion; and then having made such as are not so, and training them to be applied by Affection and Humour; so as $\frac{1}{4}$ of the whole paying needlesly four times too much, may be thereby so netled, as to do more mischief than the other unconcerned, and thankless $\frac{3}{4}$ can allay.

CHAP. VII.

The Collateral Advantages of these Taxes.

1. BEsides the equality of Taxes, we make this further use of, trying it by way of Customs, Poles, Excises, Chimney-money, Land-tax, and Assesments upon the personal Estates, *viz.*

(1.) Of the Customs, which we reduce from $\frac{1}{20}$ to $\frac{1}{50}$, to keep an account of Foreign Trade

Trade, and of its Balance; for by Levying, a Duty, and encreasing the Penalty, these Accounts will be less obscured.

(2.) The simple and universal Pole keeps an account of the great Wealth and Strength of the Kindgom, the People.

(3.) Rating the Houses *per* Chimney, gives a good account of Improvements and Dilapidations.

(4.) Excize gives an account of Domestick Expences, and publisheth Exorbitances.

(5.) Land-taxes keep the Payments to the proportion of entire value, not of Annual Rent: So as an Estate in Housing pays no more than if it were in Lands, nor considerable less than Goods, and may bring Mortgages to their just contribution; many Lenders not being so formidable for their Money, as some have thought them.

(6.) Assessments upon personal Estates (if given in as elsewhere upon Oath) would bring that Branch which of it self is most dark, to a sufficient clearness.

2. There is also a Pole upon Titles and Dignities worth consideration, tho we now omit it; which as it may check mens forwardness to undeserved Pre-eminence, so it may be employed in the encouragement of true worth.

3. We

3. We have hitherto computed the old immutable Revenue at but 130,000 *l. per annum*, nor ſuppoſed above 170,000 *l.* (*viz.* leſs than ½ what it is at preſent) to be raiſed by Cuſtoms (wholly neglecting Wards, Butlerage, Aulnage, and other obſolete Impoſts.) We have alſo deſigned the ſeveral Proportions towards the raiſing of a Million more *per Ann.* to be raiſed by the Pole, Exciſe, Land-Tax, Aſſeſſments and Chimneys.

CHAP. VIII.

Of the Expence of the Navy, Army, and Gariſons.

WE come next to ſhew, That if 3 Millions *per ann.* or 250,000 *l. per menſem* (to make up the whole 3,300,000*l. per ann.*) were raiſed, what might be performed thereby for the ſafety, eſtabliſhment, and Honour both of the King and Subject.

Unto which, I ſay, conſidering the preſent condition of the Navy, two Millions will maintain 50,000 men, in Ships of War for eight Months of the Year, and 30000 for the other four Months: Which I take to be near double the beſt Fleet we ever have

ſeen

ſeen in *Europe*, computing the Ordnance, and Harbor-Charges of the Navy: Nor will the Maintenance of 12,000 Foot, and 3000, Horſe, allowing 100,000 *l.* for Inland Gariſons, and 60,000 *l.* for *Tangier*, &c. put all together, exceed 600,000 *l.* ſo as there remains 700,000 *l.* for other Matters, whereof His Majeſty's Royal Family, by all the Accounts I have ſeen, doth not ſpend 500,000 *l.* *per ann.* Nor need the Charge of all thoſe Levies be above 1 of the 33, (*viz.* $\frac{1}{33}$ part for the 500 Officers, without ever going five Miles from the Centre of their abode) who might perform this Work; nor would more than 200 *l.* *per an.* for each of them, and their under Inſtruments be neceſſary for their reſpective Sallaries: For there are 450 Areots of 10 Miles ſquare in *England* and *Wales*.

CHAP. IX.

Motives to the quiet bearing of extraordinary TAXES.

HAving ſhewed how great and glorious things may be done with no leſs difficulty than what $\frac{1}{4}$ of the King's Subjects do already endure; I offer theſe further Reaſons

ſons to quiet mens Minds, in caſe this utmoſt 250,000 *l. per menſem* ſhould be ever demanded upon this *Holland-War*.

1. That of all Naval Expence, not $\frac{1}{20}$ is for Forreign Commodities, nor need it be ſ, if the people would do their part, and the Governours direct them the neareſt ways.

2. That ſtoppage of Trade is conſiderable, but as one to eight; for we exchange not above five Millions worth *per ann.* for our 40.

3. That the Expence of the King, *&c.* being about 400,000 *l. per ann.* is but $\frac{1}{100}$ part of the Expence of the Nation, who all have the Pleaſure and Honour of it.

4. That the Money of the Nation being but about 5 Millions and $\frac{1}{2}$, and the earning of the ſame 25; It is not difficult for them to encreaſe their Money a Million *per ann.* by an eaſie advance of their Induſtry, applyed to ſuch Manufactures as will fetch Money from abroad.

5. The Wealth of *England* lies in Land and People, ſo as they make five parts of ſix of the whole: But the Wealth of *Holland* lies more in Money, Houſing, Shipping and Wares. Now ſuppoſing *England* three-times

times as rich as *Holland* in Land, and People (as it is) and *Holland* twice as rich as we in other Particulars (as it ſcarce is); We are ſtill upon the Balance of the whole near twice as rich as they: Of which I wiſh thoſe that underſtand *Holland*, would conſider and calculate.

6. There are in *England* above four Acres of Arrable, Meadow and Paſture-Land, for every Soul in it; and thoſe ſo fertile, as that the labour of one man in tilling them, is ſufficient to get a bare Livelihood for above 10: So as 'tis for want of Diſcipline that any Poverty appears in *England*, and that any are hanged or ſtarved upon that account.

CHAP. X.

How to employ the People, and the End thereof.

WE ſaid, That half the People by a very gentle labour, might much enrich the Kingdom, and advance its Honour, by ſetting apart largely for publick uſes; But the difficulty is, upon what ſhall they employ themſelves.

To which I anſwer in general, Upon producing Food and Neceſſaries for the whole People of the Land, by few hands; whether by labouring harder, or by the introducing the Compendium, and Facilitations of Art, which is equivalent to what men vainly hoped from *Polygamy*. For as much as he that can do the Work of five men by one, effects the ſame as the begetting four adult Workmen. Nor is ſuch advantage worth fewer years purchaſe than that of Lands, or what we eſteem likeſt to perpetual. Now the making Neceſſaries cheap, by the means aforeſaid, and not by raiſing more of them than can be ſpent whilſt

whilſt they are good, will neceſſitate others to buy them with much labour of other kinds For if one man could raiſe Corn enough for the whole, better than any one man; then that man would have the natural Monopoly of Corn, and could exact more labour for it in exchange, than if ten others raiſed ten times as much Corn as is neceſſary; which would make other labour ſo much the dearer, as men were leſs under the need of engaging upon it.

2. By this way we might recover our loſt Cloth-trade, which by the ſame the *Dutch* got from us. By this way the *East-Indians* furniſh us from the other end of the world with Linnen cheaper than our ſelves can make them, with what grows at our own Doors. By this means we might fetch Flax from *France*, and yet furniſh them with Linnen (that is) if we make no more than we can vend, but ſo much with the feweſt hands, and cheapeſt food, which will be when Food alſo is raiſed, by fewer hands than elſewhere.

3. I anſwer generally we ſhould employ our ſelves by raiſing ſuch Commodities, as would yield and fetch in money from abroad: For that would ſupply any wants of ours from the ſame, or any other place at all times. Which Stores of Domeſtick

ſtick Commodities could not effect, whoſe value is to call a Temporary (*i. e.*) which are of value but *pro hic & nunc.*

4. But when ſhould we reſt from this great Induſtry? I anſwer, When we have certainly more Money than any of our Neighbour States, (though never ſo little) both in Arithmetrical and Geometrical proportion (*i. e.*) when we have more years proviſion aforehand, and more preſent effects.

5. What then ſhould we buſie our ſelves about? I anſwer, in Ratiocinations upon the Works and Will of God, to be ſupported not only by the indolency, but alſo by the pleaſure of the Body; and not only by the tranquility, but ſerenity of the mind; and this Exerciſe is the natural end of man in this world, and that which beſt diſpoſeth him for his Spiritual happineſs in that other which is to come. The motions of the mind being the quickeſt of all others, afford moſt variety, wherein is the very form and being of pleaſure; and by how much the more we have of this pleaſure, by ſo much the more we are capable of it even *ad Infinitum.*

FINIS.